21.10

EVANSTON PUBLIC LIBRARY

3 1192 00809 7881

x943 Spenc.W

Spencer, William, 1922-

Germany then and now /

NOV 0 8 1995

D1569807

GERMANY
THEN AND NOW

GERMANY

THEN AND NOW

WILLIAM SPENCER

FRANKLIN WATTS
New York   Chicago   London   Toronto   Sydney

EVANSTON PUBLIC LIBRARY
CHILDREN'S DEPARTMENT
1703 ORRINGTON AVENUE
EVANSTON, ILLINOIS 60201

Map by Gary S. Tong
Photographs copyright ©: UPI/Bettmann Newsphotos: pp. 10, 19, 90, 99,
103, 110, 115, 119, 123; Archive Photos, NYC: pp. 16 (Berech), 113;
Reuters/Bettmann Newsphotos: pp. 20, 137, 140, 146; The Bettmann
Archives: pp. 27, 54, 63, 68, 77, 97; Library of Congress: pp. 29, 86; New
York Public Library, Picture Collection: pp. 32, 40, 48, 57, 83, 106; Wide
World Photos: pp. 52, 134; Bettman / Hulton Newsphotos: p. 66 bottom; The
National Archives: pp. 70, 74; Impact Visuals: pp. 127 (Donna Binder), 143
(Teit Hornbak).

Library of Congress Cataloging-in-Publication Data

Spencer, William, 1922–
Germany then and now / William Spencer
p.   cm.
Includes bibliographical references and index.
ISBN 0-531-11137-7
1. Germany—History—Juvenile literature   [1. Germany—History.]
I. Title
DD89.s68   1993
943—dc20   93-29444
                                                         CIP AC

Copyright © 1994 by William Spencer
All rights reserved
Printed in the United States of America
6 5 4 3 2 1

To John A. Bouvier III, brother,
supporter, and valued friend, and the
very embodiment of *gemütlichkeit*
in an unstable world

And, as always, for Elizabeth

CONTENTS

GERMANY
THEN AND NOW

The Berlin Wall was constructed in 1961,
dividing an ancient city into two parts. Here,
in a residential area, several lines of
barbed wire on the eastern side make even
an approach to the Wall impossible.

PROLOGUE

All that we know who lie in gaol*
Is that the wall is strong;
And that each day is like a year,
A year whose days are long.
—Oscar Wilde,
The Ballad of Reading Gaol

On a sunny Sunday morning in August 1961, a group of children gathered near the entrance to the Tiergarten, a large park in the middle of the city of Berlin, Germany. The Tiergarten, like Central Park in New York City, has woods, jogging paths, riding trails, ponds, and playgrounds. It is a wonderful place for children of all ages. On that Sunday morning, this particular group of friends gathered there as was their custom. Their homes were nearby, and they had been coming to the Tiergarten since they were old enough to walk. Even before then, their mothers had wheeled them in their baby carriages across a wide street and into the park. The Tiergarten was an important part of their lives.

*Gaol is the Old English spelling for *jail*.

There was, in 1961, one big difference between New York's Central Park and the Tiergarten. People who lived in New York, whether on the West Side of Manhattan or the East, could either walk or take the subway or bus to the park. All New Yorkers have always been free to use its facilities. But in 1961, as it would be until 1989, Berlin was a divided city under two governments. When children from the eastern part of the city went to the Tiergarten, they had to cross an international border because East and West Berlin, two halves of the same city, belonged to two different countries.

These two countries are today one country, the Federal Republic of Germany, with Berlin—undivided Berlin—as the capital of that country. But for forty years (1949–1989) the German people lived under the rule of two separate governments. One of them was the Federal Republic of Germany (FRG), usually called West Germany. The other, a much smaller part of German territory, was the German Democratic Republic (Deutsche Demokratische Republik, or DDR), called East Germany. To make matters more confusing, East Berlin was the capital of the DDR, while West Berlin, although surrounded by East Germany, was part of West Germany.

This situation arose as the result of World War II, which lasted from 1939 to 1945. The war began when German armies invaded Poland, Germany's eastern neighbor. Other German invasions brought most of Europe under German control. The German occupation was marked by great cruelty and mistreatment of conquered peoples, particularly the Jewish population of the occupied countries. In 1941 the German government of Adolf Hitler began a systematic campaign of extermination of European Jews, an action it called the "Final Solution" because in the minds of Hitler and his associates Jews were responsible for Germany's previous war losses and economic problems and had been a "problem" for Christian Germans for centuries. Some 6 million Jews were rounded up, taken to concentration camps, and later executed by firing squads or other means or, in most cases, asphyxiated in gas chambers. (The term "the Holocaust" is more commonly used to describe the deaths of the 6 million because of the use of crematoria to burn the dead victims.) Millions of other Europeans— especially Poles, Russians, Czechs, and other Slavic peoples considered racially inferior by Hitler's government— went to their deaths in similar fashion.

Germany surrendered in 1945 to the combined armies of Great Britain, France, the United States, and the Soviet Union. The victors were determined that the Germans should never again become a threat to the peace of Europe and the world. But due to political differences, they could not agree on how this should be done. The United States, Britain, and France wanted to set up a democratic form of government in Germany, so that once Germany had paid for its sins it could rejoin the family of peace-loving nations. The goal of the Soviet Union (which had suffered heavily under German occupation) was to prevent the rise of a united Germany allied with the Western democracies. As a result, Germany was divided into two zones of occupation, one controlled by the Western powers and the other by the Soviet Army. In 1949, the Western powers set up the FRG, and in response the Soviet Union established the DDR in its zone. As was noted earlier, the Soviet occupation left Berlin entirely surrounded by East German territory, but West Berlin remained a part of the FRG, with troops of the Western powers stationed there under the 1945 four-power agreement that ended the war.

These momentous events had relatively little effect on the children of Berlin. Up until 1961, East and West Berlin children alike mixed and played freely in the Tiergarten. For the children of East Berlin in particular, the park was a bright spot in their drab lives. Many of them lived in cramped apartments; as often as they could, they escaped to its fresh air, trees, grass, and swings. The West German guards in their green uniforms usually smiled as they waved them across the border, while the East German Vopos (Volkspolizei, or "People's Police") simply ignored them. On that sunny August Sunday they chattered excitedly as they waited for a break in the traffic and then darted like tiny swallows across Reinhartstrasse, skipping happily toward the park entrance.

But something unexpected happened on that Sunday, something that changed the lives of those East German children and their families in ways they could not foresee. When the children reached the park entrance, they found it closed. Guards told them to go home. Down the street the Brandenburg Gate, historic entrance to the old city, was being sealed shut by grim-faced East German workmen. As the children stumbled in a daze back across Reinhartstrasse, now empty of traffic, other workmen began building a high wall along the border between East and West Berlin. Within a short time, the wall stretched right across the middle of the city, eventually reaching more than 100 miles (160 km) in length as it was wrapped around all of West Berlin. East German leaders referred to it in speeches as the "antifascist protective barrier," as if they had built it to shield their own people from Western democratic ideas and influences.

The Berlin Wall (der Mauer, as Germans on both sides called it) was not only a political and psychological barrier but also a physical one, an obstacle to East Germans trying to escape to West Germany and freedom from Communist rule. It was strong and thick, 12 to 13 feet (3.7–4 m) high, built of ugly grayish-brown concrete blocks. The Wall cut streets crossing Berlin from east to west literally in two; at one point railway tracks ended in midair over a trestle. In place of the closed Brandenburg Gate, a new entry point, called Checkpoint Charlie,[1] was set up at a nearby corner of Friedrichstrasse, another major artery. Checkpoint Charlie consisted of two cinder block police booths, lit up at night in the harsh glare of yellow spotlights and shielded from chill rains by a corrugated metal canopy. For visitors to East Berlin, it was the only legal entry point.

As we will see later in this book, the Berlin Wall marked a turning point in the Cold War that had developed between the United States and the Soviet Union after World War II. But for the young people of East Berlin it had a more personal impact—it was as if their own government had walled them in, into a prison of its own making. A high school student recalled that "my parents . . . talked . . . in hushed tones about World War II,"[2] and one of the children who had been barred from the Tiergarten told her mother angrily, "Now we'll never get out of here!"[3]

In the years that followed, the Berlin Wall came to symbolize the division of Europe into free democratic nations with elected governments, and those dominated by Communist governments subordinate to the Soviet Union. The Wall's immediate purpose, the reason it had been built in such a hurry, was to stop the flight of Eastern Europeans to the West. Between 1945 and 1961, about 3 million had fled, over half through West Berlin, and by mid-1961 the number of escapees had reached almost 2,000 a day. They included many of the people who were most needed to develop the German Democratic Republic: doctors, engineers, architects, skilled workers, nurses, lawyers, and business managers.

With der Mauer in place, it became much harder for East Germans to escape from their own country. They attempted in all sorts of ways to cross it. Some climbed over the Wall, while others dug tunnels underneath. One man built an airplane on the roof of his apartment

building and flew over the Wall. A young woman escaped when she was smuggled through Checkpoint Charlie hidden in two lashed-together suitcases in a car trunk; one side had been cut out of each suitcase to provide the necessary space. By the time the Wall came tumbling down in 1989, over 200 people had died in efforts to cross it, children as well as adults.

It is said that one gets used to misfortune, if there seems to be no alternative; and in time people on both sides of the Wall came to terms with it. Joggers said they liked to run there because there was no traffic and the air was pretty good. On the West Berlin side, homeowners living nearby set up Ping-Pong tables and picnic areas and planted flower beds, as if to show their neighbors across the Wall what life could be like in a free society. By the time of its twenty-fifth anniversary, in 1986, der Mauer had become a tourist attraction. Tourists came by the busload to see it, and hot-dog stands and souvenir shops did a brisk business.

Most Germans also came to believe that the Wall would be there for a very long time, perhaps forever. They became convinced that the two Germanys would never be reunited, and most experts agreed with them. There was too much hatred of Germany in Europe after two world wars to allow reunification to take place. East Germany's leaders declared that the Wall was necessary

A border guard paces the narrow artery open between East Berlin (to the left of the white line) and West Berlin at Checkpoint Charlie.

to protect their people from their enemies and from the corruption of Western democracy. Early in 1989 the head of the German Democratic Republic, Erich Honecker, said in a speech that the Wall would last 100 years, and a survey found that the majority of the West German people agreed with him. Four decades of Communism in East Germany and democratic government in West Germany had made the two German peoples so different from each other that it was generally believed that unity under a single government would not work even if the rest of Europe allowed it to happen.

In the decade of the 1990s we know that the experts, Erich Honecker, the West German people, and most of the world were wrong. The final returns are not in, but the two Germanys are reunited for better or worse under one government. Once again, children from East Berlin, the children and grandchildren of the group turned away from the Tiergarten on that long-ago August Sunday, may play happily in the park—there is no Wall in their way now. Like Humpty Dumpty, der Mauer came tumbling down in November 1989, a few short months after Honecker had predicted a long life for it.

Yet the past is always prologue. The Germany of today has roots that go back 2,000 years and more, to a time when fierce Germanic tribes roamed the forests and

While a good number of people managed to escape from East Berlin despite the Wall, many others—including this young man shot by East German police—died in the effort.

18

Experiment „Sozialismus"
ehr mit uns
Wolf
WIR SIND EIN VOLK
Berlin

swamps of central Europe. German history has evolved in a particular place, through experiences that molded a distinctive German character and values and shaped a particular German culture.

From the first contacts of these tribespeople with the forces of law, order, and civilization as represented by Rome, to the invasions of World War II, Germany's relations with its European neighbors have often been difficult. The years since World War II have been marked by a mellowing of German character and a modification of German behavior that have helped to lessen the fears of these neighbors of a revival of German aggressiveness. Now the German nation is unified again, but a new and powerful Germany that is emerging in a Europe itself moving toward unity and the breaking-down of borders still worries Germany's neighbors. Can we trust them? Ask the French, the Poles, the Dutch, the victims of Hitler's tyranny. A look at German history—the history of what one author calls "the retarded nation," one never exposed to political education through the English or the American Enlightenment—offers some clues, but not a final answer.

At a December 1989
demonstration in support
of reunification,
East Germans express
their feeling:
"We are one people."

ONE

THE GERMANS AND THEIR SPACE

What is the German Fatherland?
Wherever the German tongue is heard.
—Ernst Moritz Arndt, 1813

Germany is the largest country in central Europe, with a land area of 137,740 square miles (356,750 sq km). The population (in 1990) was 78 million, 61 million in the former Federal Republic (West Germany) and 17 million in the ex–German Democratic Republic (East Germany). Due to its central location, Germany shares borders with nine other European countries. The border with France lies along the historic Rhine, one of Europe's busiest rivers. The lands along both banks of the Rhine have shifted back and forth between German and French control over the centuries, but the boundary today is a peaceful one as river barges and tourist excursion boats move north and south through its murky waters.

Germany's eastern border, with Poland, is the so-called Oder-Neisse line, demarcated by the Oder and

Neisse rivers. This border was also much fought over in the past, but in June 1990 a formal peace treaty between Poland and the new Federal Republic confirmed the line as permanent. Germany's other borders are with Belgium, Holland, and Denmark to the north, the Czech and Slovak republics, Switzerland, and Austria to the south. This central location has been important in German history—especially in the long struggle for German unity.

The Germans' space is made up of three distinct geographical regions: north, central, and south. Northern Germany has a deeply indented coastline extending inland from the North and Baltic seas. The major seaports, Hamburg and Bremen, are located some distance inland from the sea but along navigable rivers. These rivers, the Elbe, Weser, Oder, and Neisse, spread like fingers across the north German plain, broad rolling country that stretches unchanged across Poland and into Russia as far as the Ural Mountains.

Central Germany is more varied in its terrain, ranging from the rugged, once heavily forested region east of the Rhine to the level plains that extend toward the Czech border. Small mountain areas and rugged hills serve to break up this terrain, with towns and cities that still retain a medieval appearance with their castles and half-timbered houses. The majority of medium-sized German cities, such as Leipzig, Frankfurt, Dresden, and Nuremburg, are located in this region.

Southern Germany, which includes the ancient kingdom of Bavaria and the Grand Duchy of Württemberg, is geographically a world apart from the rest of the country. It consists of a heavily forested high plateau, with rugged mountains that extend south to link up with the Alps, Europe's highest range.

Industrialization and urban growth have brought many changes to the German landscape as well as to German life. But much of the country is not vastly different in appearance from what it was a century ago, perhaps due to the German passion for preserving nature and their love of order and tradition. A nineteenth-century German naturalist, Wilhelm Riehl, described it as a land "of wide streambeds, extensive marshlands, and tiny hamlets; imposing lakes and ponds; countless hills, as indistinguishable from each other as the waves of the sea. . . . throughout these regions one has the impression of ample space, space enough for a population twice its present size."[1] A more recent visitor noted: "The countryside barely changed, but I had an indeterminate feeling of having traveled back in time. . . . Someone had built a wooden pylon near his house and set a wagon wheel on it, where a pair of storks had built their nest. . . . I noticed cobbled streets in the villages, where there had been tarmac in the West, and red-brick houses with high gables. . . ."[2]

The idea of *space*, a particular space that belongs to them, is very important to the German people. Germany has been a unified nation under a single central government for only a short time. But the German sense of belonging to a place that is particularly *German* dates back several thousand years, ever since the first Germanic tribes wandered into central Europe and claimed a portion of it for themselves. The German word *innerlichkeit* ("innerness") expresses this special German feeling of living in a particular space inhabited by and sensitive to the German soul. Even those Germans who migrated to other European countries in the nineteenth and twentieth centuries, or were caught up in the upheavals of war and became refugees, held on to this special feeling. With the breakup of the Soviet Union in 1991–92, for example, residents of German communities in the former Soviet republics who had spent their lives outside Germany began to migrate to the new German Federal Republic, a land most of them had never seen.

German space, and the independent spirit of Germanic tribes, were first tested some 2,000 years ago when armies of the Roman Empire invaded central Europe. In A.D. 9, three Roman legions entered the vast Teutoburg Forest (Teutoburger Wald) on a mission to bring these tribes under Roman rule. As they moved deeper and deeper into the dark forest, they were ambushed by German warriors in a surprise attack and killed almost to the last man. The German leader, Hermann (called Arminius by the Roman chroniclers of the period), is considered the first genuine German national hero. A large part of the Teutoburger Wald still stands, even after 2,000 years of use, as a reminder to modern Germans of the time their ancestors destroyed a Roman army. To this day, German children learn about the exploits of Hermann, chief of the Cherusci tribe, in their textbooks.

One important difference between the Germans and other western European peoples lies in the fact that the Germans were never ruled by Romans. Roman armies made no further efforts to conquer the lands east of the Rhine and north of the Danube. The territory beyond these rivers was unknown to them, a vast area "bristling with forest and reeking with swamps," to use the colorful language of the Roman historian Tacitus. Other Europeans received the benefits of Roman civilization, Roman law, and the protection of Roman legions, and wrote and spoke Latin, unlike the German tribes with their unwritten languages and dialects. The Romans referred

Victorious over the invading Roman legions, German warriors honor their leader, Hermann.

to the Germans as *barbarei* ("barbarians") because they knew no Latin. However, when the Roman Empire weakened and its borders were no longer defended, various Germanic tribes began to move across these borders and establish settlements, farming the land, learning Latin, and becoming Roman subjects themselves. When the Roman Empire broke up, in the fifth century A.D., chiefs of the more powerful tribes formed their own independent kingdoms. Several of these kingdoms are the ancestors of modern European nations. Perhaps the most important such kingdom was that of the Franks, the ancestors of modern France, although it included a much larger area than present-day France. In A.D. 800 the Frankish king, Carolus, made a pilgrimage to Rome to seek the support of the pope. In return for pledges of fealty and support, the pope crowned him "Carolus Magnus [Charlemagne], the Emperor of Rome."

Charlemagne's goal was to revive the Roman Empire, now called the Holy Roman Empire because it was closely tied to the Roman Catholic Church and ruled by Charlemagne, at least in theory, on behalf of the pope. During his brief reign (A.D. 800–814), the lands he governed included most of France plus western Germany, Switzerland, Austria, Belgium, Holland, and northern Italy. Unfortunately, his empire did not survive his death. According to his will, it was divided among his three grandsons. One of them, Otto of Saxony, who had received northern Germany and Austria as his inheritance, went to Rome and had himself crowned "Holy Roman Emperor of the German Nation" in 962. From that time until the early 1800s, the Holy Roman Empire of the German Nation provided a semblance of a central government for the German people.

However, the empire's survival depended upon support from landowning nobles and princes who had their own military forces. The emperors made a practice of

By A.D. 800, Charlemagne had created an
empire that stretched from the region of
central Italy north to Denmark, and from
eastern Germany west to the Atlantic Ocean.

granting lands and titles to these nobles and tribal chiefs in return for pledges of loyalty and promises to contribute troops to the empire's defense in times of danger. As a result, the land of the German nation became a crazy quilt of sovereign states, dukedoms, principalities, free cities, and the like, each one ruled by a sovereign jealous of all rivals and often in conflict with them.

In the thirteenth century, the Holy Roman Empire was weakened even further when the Habsburg family, Swiss landowners, claimed the throne and the right to name all future emperors. This action set off a series of large and small wars between them and other rulers who rejected Habsburg authority. Much of this conflict took place on German soil. While England, France, and other European countries were moving toward rule by a single central monarchy, Germany remained a hotbed of warring rulers.

Despite the wars and political instability, there were certain factors that worked to draw the German people together as a nation. One of them was language. A unified German language gradually replaced Latin as the language of the courts and trade. It took two forms, High German, used by the nobility, and Low German, the language of the people. However the two forms sprang from the same roots, and either form could be understood by the other group. Martin Luther, the founder of Protestantism and thus an important figure in German history, once remarked: "I use the common German language so that both High and Low Germans may understand me equally well."[3]

The Germans' sense of themselves as belonging to a particular nation was also strengthened by their life-style. Most of them lived in villages or small, compact towns or cities that were usually walled. Except for occasional trips to distant cities for trade, or pilgrimages to religious centers such as Rome, they rarely traveled far from their homes, spending their entire lives in the same place and often in the same house in which they had been born. They grew their own food and were largely self-sufficient, with craftsmen of all kinds available to take care of the few things they could not do themselves. Most trades were organized into guilds, rather like modern labor unions; each guild provided protection for its members, maintained quality standards, and represented the membership in its dealings with local rulers and even with the emperor himself.

Another factor that helped to strengthen the feeling of the Germans of belonging to a particular nation was the organization of cities, especially seaports, into leagues to carry on foreign trade. The most important league was the Hanse, or Hanseatic League. Its members, notably the cities of Hamburg, Bremen, and Lübeck, controlled the empire's trade; in return, the emperor recognized them as independent, self-governing cities under their own city councils. Merchants of the Hanse cities became wealthy through foreign trade, and their tall three-masted ships ranged as far as Iceland, the Baltic, and the Mediterranean during the Middle Ages, exchanging the products of the empire for those of other countries. The grand palaces and tall half-timbered houses of Hanseatic merchants, although overshadowed today by industrial plants and grimy with pollution, still stand in Germany's seaports as visible reminders for young Germans of a time when their nation was a world-trade leader.

THE REFORMATION

The prosperity, order, and relative tranquillity that Germans had enjoyed in the Middle Ages under indirect imperial rule and the trade dominance of the Hanseatic League were shattered in the sixteenth century. Germany, like most of Europe, was predominantly Catholic, and over the years the Catholic Church not only dominated public and private life but also grew rich through the sale of "indulgences"—favors by which a believer

Among his other achievements, Martin Luther,
the German religious reformer, translated
the New Testament from Greek into German.
Here he is seen lecturing at the
University of Wittenberg.

could "buy" salvation and a place in heaven in return for gifts or special contributions over and above the required tenth-of-income tithe. In time, many Christians came to believe that the practice was wrong, especially because cathedrals and churches all over Europe were filled with gold objects, silver, jewelry, brass ornaments, and even chinaware, donated by rich and poor alike in hopes of finding favor with God. But no one had the courage to question the practice until an unknown monk named Martin Luther nailed a list of ninety-five Complaints Against the Church to the door of the main church in Wittenberg in 1517.

Luther argued in his Complaints that salvation, or forgiveness from sin, was possible only through the grace of God, who might or might not grant it. Neither good works nor pious behavior, nor especially gifts to the Church, were absolute guarantees of a place in heaven.

Other "complaints" of Luther were that Christians should be allowed to worship according to their own consciences and not be told *how* to worship by priests and other Church officials, and that the idea that only the Church and its leaders could mediate between a person and God was wrong.

Luther's action enraged the Church fathers. He was expelled from his monastic order and was excommunicated, a terrible thing in those days when the Church literally had the power of life and death over its members. But, as noted, many Christians were angry about the methods used by the Church to achieve financial gain. They joined Luther in protesting Catholic Church policies, and as a result, a new religious movement called Lutheranism and later Protestantism was formed in Germany and soon spread throughout Europe.

Unfortunately for the German people in particular, an essentially religious dispute soon escalated into a general war, as European rulers seized opportunities to expand their territories at the expense of their rivals.

French, Austrian, Swedish, and other armies converged on Germany, and due to its central location, the country became a battleground. For thirty years (1618–1648), Germans suffered the horrors of war. When the rulers of Europe finally grew tired of conflict and made peace, the German countryside lay in ruins. In a foretaste of twentieth-century wars, the civilian population suffered even more than the soldiers of the various armies. Towns and villages were burned to the ground, crops were destroyed, and thousands of people died from epidemic diseases such as typhoid fever. A German poet wrote:

> *The towers stand in flames, the church is*
> *overturned,*
> *The town hall lies in ruins, the stalwart are*
> *hacked to bits, . . .*
> *Fire, plague and death oppress the heart and soul.*[4]

The German playwright Bertolt Brecht, in his great play *Mother Courage and Her Children*, described the scene graphically: "Those who are spared in battle die by plague. Over once blooming countryside hunger rages. . . . Wolves prowl the empty streets."

Almost 350 years have passed since the Thirty Years' War ended, and it is almost impossible to imagine the plague raging or wolves roaming the streets of the crowded, tidy, and prosperous German cities of today. But in terms of Germany's slow growth toward political unity as a nation, that war may be compared with our Civil War—only in reverse. The Treaty of Westphalia, unlike Lee's surrender at Appomattox, left the Holy Roman Empire intact under Austrian Habsburg rule. But it also sanctioned the division of Germany into over 300 separate sovereign states, each subject to the emperor in theory but actually independent of him, and of each other.

THE LAND
IN THE
MIDDLE

England is an empire, France is a person,
Germany is a nation, a race.
—Jules Michelet,
Histoire de France

The end of the Thirty Years' War brought peace to the
people but very little else—their farms had been destroyed, crop production had been severely curtailed, the
population had been drastically reduced by war, famine,
and disease. As a result, Germany became what one
author calls the "retarded nation," unable to develop the
political institutions and limits on the powers of absolute
monarchy that had enabled other European countries,
notably France and England, to become more democratic. It seemed to most Germans that they had very
little control over their own destinies. The future was in
the hands of outsiders, European rulers who had divided
their land into petty states, each ruled by a prince who
considered himself a sovereign in his own territory.

A second result of the war seemed to have been a

noticeable growth in certain attitudes and character traits that most outsiders—and the Germans themselves—think of when they are describing a behavior pattern that is particularly German. One such attitude is blind obedience to authority. This trait may have older roots—a pope in the Middle Ages called Germany "the land of obedience"[1]—but the horrors of war and the daily experience of death certainly made those who survived more willing to accept whatever authority seemed capable of protecting them from further misery. The local German rulers, along with the Church (Catholic or Protestant, it made no difference), provided such protection, asking only obedience in return. The Württemberg publisher Karl Friedrich Moser, a keen observer of German life, was to write a century later: "Every nation has its principal motive. In Germany, it is obedience; in England, freedom; in Holland, trade; in France, the honor of the King."[2]

This main German character trait, along with others that have been refined over centuries of interaction, such as love of order, and love of cleanliness, led to the emergence in the eighteenth century of one small German state that became the leader of the others. It would also eventually be the driving force behind Germany's first unification as a nation. This small state was Prussia.

THE RISE OF PRUSSIA

Prussia's early history was quite different from that of other German states. It was also "off center" in the "Land in the Middle" (central Europe), being located far to the east, along what is today the Polish border and farther eastward. The region had no particular identity and was populated largely by tribes from farther north, near the Baltic Sea. They were farmers and herders and were pagan in religion, worshiping spirits and natural forces. But in the thirteenth century, the Prussian tribes were conquered and forced to convert to Christianity by the Teutonic Knights, an order of warrior-monks. The knights ruled at first from a chain of fortified castles on high ground east of the Elbe River. In time they became landowners, ruling vast estates farmed for them by the conquered peoples as serfs or tenant farmers. The descendants of the knights formed a military nobility, the Junkers ("country squires").

Once they had conquered the region, these Junkers spent most of their time hunting, and riding over their estates to supervise their farmers and herdsmen. But the militaristic spirit that had brought them there awaited only an opportunity to resurface. That opportunity came in the late 1600s, when a prominent Junker family joined in marriage with the Hohenzollerns, rulers of the small duchy of Brandenburg. The Hohenzollern capital was a dusty garrison town named Berlin. The dukes of Brandenburg saw a chance to expand their duchy with the support of the Prussian Junkers, while the possibilities for military action encouraged many young Prussian aristocrats, particularly younger sons, to head for Berlin and enroll in the armies of the duke.

It is important to note here, for Germany's future as well as its past, that two elements often at odds have dominated German character. One is this spirit of militarism, which when turned to aggression has led the nation into two great wars and in past centuries has kept the Germans embroiled with their neighbors in numerous small ones.

The other element is best described by the German word *Gemütlichkeit*, meaning coziness, a warm homey atmosphere, gentleness and kindness, a "neighborliness." It is a good description of the homey, intimate, close-knit family life-style of German towns and villages before the Thirty Years' War, and slowly restored after that war. The great German composer Richard Wagner spoke of gemütlichkeit in an essay in terms that would strike a chord in German hearts today: "After the . . . destruction . . . it was this most intimately homely world . . . from which the German spirit was reborn."[3]

Unfortunately for Germany's future as a united nation, the militaristic spirit that predominated in Brandenburg-Prussia rather than the gemütlichkeit of other German societies came to dominate German policy and behavior. By the mid-1700s Prussia, no longer Brandenburg, had become a leading power in Europe. Although small in territory, it had an efficient, well-trained, disciplined army tested in battle and ready for conquest. Prussia's major rival was Austria. The Habsburg emperors felt they had a right to the leadership of all German states; after all, they were still Holy Roman Emperors of the German nation. Other European powers feared Prussian expansionism. In 1756, French, Russian, and Austrian armies invaded Prussia. However, the Prussian army managed to keep them at bay despite heavy odds. Prussia's king, Frederick Wilhelm II (1740–1786), became a national hero to all Germans because of his successful defense of German territory.

This war, which began in 1756, ended with a peace treaty in 1763. For this reason, it is naturally called the Seven Years' War in European history. Prussia not only held on to its own territory but added some at the expense of Austria and neighboring Poland. The latter country was divided up among Prussia, Russia, and Austria and ceased to exist as a nation for 150 years. Frederick Wilhelm II also took over the lands of several small German states, making Prussia the largest state in Germany.

EFFECT OF THE
FRENCH REVOLUTION

Prussia's leadership and the movement toward German unity were severely tested during the French Revolution of 1789. The overthrow and execution of the French king, and the establishment of a "people's government" in France committed to the ideals of liberty, equality, and fraternity (brotherhood), stirred much of the world, but initially aroused little interest among the German people. But when France's revolutionary leaders called upon other European peoples to rise up and overthrow their rulers, the powers of Europe took notice. They sent armies to crush the revolution. By 1792, France was at war with the rest of Europe.

At this critical juncture in France's history, an unknown young officer from the Mediterranean island of Corsica was given command of French troops and demonstrated his military skill by winning several battles. To the revolutionary leaders, quarreling among themselves over power, the young officer seemed the savior of France. He was named first consul (the equivalent of prime minister) in 1799. His name was Napoleon Bonaparte.

Napoleon proved to be a true military genius, winning victory after victory over Prussian, Austrian, and other European armies and in the process writing his name in large letters in history. In 1804 a grateful population saluted him as emperor of France. The new French empire included all of Germany, in fact, all of Europe west of the Elbe. Napoleon organized his German territories into a "Confederation of the Rhine," ruled by his brother Jerome as king of Westphalia. In 1806 the defeated Austrian ruler, Francis II, agreed to give up the title of Holy Roman Emperor in return for peace, and the thousand-year-old empire founded by Charlemagne was finally laid to rest.

In theory, the Confederation of the Rhine represented the interests of the German people, but in practice it proved a heavy burden. French authorities imposed heavy taxes on German cities to pay the costs of war and occupation. Young Germans were rounded up by the thousands and forced to serve in Napoleon's armies; many

In 1804 Napoleon crowned himself emperor
and ordered a portrait in coronation robes.
In the following years he extended his realm
so that, by 1812, his empire covered most of
Europe—including the Confederation of the
Rhine and much of northern Germany.

were killed or wounded fighting the battles of another country, in some cases against their own people.

In 1812, Napoleon made what would prove to be a fatal mistake. Organizing a huge "Grand Army," which included Prussian and other German troops along with his seasoned French veterans, he led his men across German territory in an invasion of Russia, the last area of Europe (except for the island nation England) not under French control. But as Germany's twentieth-century leader Adolf Hitler would do in the Second World War, Napoleon and his generals underestimated the Russian winter, the fierceness of the Russians' defense of sacred "Mother Russia," and the scorched-earth tactics of retreating Russian armies who, in order to deny food and shelter to the French forces, destroyed crops and burned villages as they retreated.

As the battered remnants of Napoleon's Grand Army retreated across German territory, the Germans rose up to fight what is still known in German historical memory as the War of Liberation. German snipers harried the French retreat, while a coalition of mainly Prussian and English armies was formed to finally rid Europe of the domination of the French emperor. Napoleon's luck ran out in 1815, in a field near the small Belgian village of Waterloo, a name that still symbolizes complete and utter defeat. The emperor was bundled off under heavy guard into exile on the remote British Atlantic island of St. Helena, where he died under mysterious circumstances some years later. With his passing, all European peoples, but especially the Germans, breathed a collective sigh of relief.

THE CONGRESS OF VIENNA

In 1815 the European powers met at Vienna, the Austrian capital, to set peace terms for France and reestablish the European power structure as it had existed before

Napoleon's time and even before the French Revolution. Each of the major powers was determined to limit the power of the others to either wage war or dominate the politics of the European continent. As a result a "balance of power" was established among the competing interests of rulers. Austria and Prussia in particular were in competition for control of German territory. The Congress of Vienna confirmed the Austrian Habsburg emperor as head of a "new" German confederation of thirty-eight principalities, dukedoms, free cities, and kingdoms, *including* the kingdom of Prussia.

But the new ideas of liberty, equality, and brotherhood of the French Revolution were not so easily put aside. In Germany especially, young people in the years after 1815 seized on these ideas with enthusiasm. Many of them were angry that the old system of many small states ruled by absolute sovereigns had been perpetuated by the European powers at the Congress of Vienna. These young people were determined that the German nation should control its own destiny. A student movement called Young Germany was formed to lead a campaign to oust German local rulers and establish a unified Germany. Young Germany organized demonstrations, passing out leaflets that demanded equality under the law for men and women, freedom of the press and education, protection of minorities, and a constitution that would set limits on the absolute power of rulers.

THE "REVOLUTION" OF 1848

As the activities of the Young Germany movement expanded, the various German rulers began to take action. Demonstrations were broken up, student leaders beaten and jailed. The black-, red-, and gold-striped Prussian flag, designed by a young girl to inspire resistance to the French occupation, was banned from use after a large crowd with arms linked marched through city streets singing "from the black present through blood to a golden future" in a mockery of its colors. Violence grew steadily, with more and more arrests and with officials in some German states being beaten or even killed.

The same thing began to happen throughout Europe as people everywhere rose up against the tyranny of absolute rulers. People's expectations and hopes for democracy soared as these rulers suddenly seemed to give way. In Germany, representatives from all German states and all levels of society met in Frankfurt to form an all-German Diet (parliament). There they drafted a constitution "for the German nation." In keeping with tradition, the government would be a constitutional monarchy. The Diet's representatives offered the crown to King Frederick Wilhelm IV of Prussia. The king had already accepted, in principle, a power-sharing arrangement; in a speech earlier in Berlin he had said: "From now on, Prussia is part of Germany."[4]

But the "revolution" against absolutism was not to be a successful one. Prussia's king had felt himself under pressure to make concessions to democracy, especially as rulers all over Europe seemed about to be overthrown. Now he moved to crush democracy by force. The power of the state and its military forces were too much for the revolutionaries, and slowly but surely the old order was restored. Frederick Wilhelm IV spurned the crown when it was offered to him by members of the Diet. "I am king by the grace of God," he said. "A crown is only fit for a pig when it is offered me by the people."[5] His troops surrounded the meeting hall and forced the Diet to adjourn, as Germany's first experiment with constitutional government came to a swift end.

The 1848 "revolution" failed in Germany as elsewhere because absolute rulers held military power over their subjects and their armies remained loyal. But in Germany the democratic movement was divided by many important issues. Some Germans wanted to establish a nation of all German-speaking peoples. Others preferred a "lesser Germany" (*Kleindeutschland*) of the German states with Prussia included but Austria excluded. Socialists, who urged a better distribution of wealth among all classes, clashed with merchants, who wanted to hold on to their hereditary privileges. Royalists argued that the only legitimate system of rule was one based on the divine right of kings, while others called for a classless state in which workers held power.

Despite its failure, however, the attempt to revolutionize European politics had three important results for the German nation. First, Prussia's future was linked definitively to that of the German states. Second, the future Germany would be a Kleindeutschland, excluding Austria with its large non-German ethnic groups. And third, 1848 provided German nationalists with a symbol, one that was set to music. In 1841 a writer of church hymns, August Heinrich Hoffman von Fallersleben, had written an anthem which he entitled "Deutschland über Alles." The famed composer Franz Joseph Haydn came across it, liked the words, and wrote new music to match its stirring lyrics. These lyrics, which spoke of "unity, justice, freedom for Germany above all," mirrored the feelings of those who had fought to establish democracy in the "Land in the Middle," and it became Germany's national anthem.

T H R E E

UNITY—BY IRON AND BLOOD

The great questions of the time are not
decided by speeches and majority
decisions ... but by iron and blood.
—Otto von Bismarck,
Speech to the Diet, 1862

With the failure of the 1848 "revolution," the way was
clear for a leader made of "iron and blood" to complete
the process of uniting the German states into a single
powerful German nation. As history often shows, a great
leader may emerge at a critical time. The nineteenth-
century Industrial Revolution had not passed Germany
by; German industries were well established, German
cities like Berlin were becoming modernized rapidly, and
German ports did a brisk trade with the rest of the world.
But due to its political disunity the country lagged behind
its European rivals, particularly France and England, in
economic development. England, with its overseas colonies, its naval power, and its access to sources of raw
materials in Africa and Asia, had a great advantage over
Germany.

The leader who appeared to unify the German nation and lead it to greatness was a Prussian aristocrat, Otto von Bismarck-Schönhausen. He was a true Junker, the offspring of two families prominent in Prussia for centuries. His maternal grandfather had been a high official at the Court of Frederick Wilhelm II, and his father owned large estates that had been in the family since the 1300s.

Bismarck's mother, as befitted the daughter of a court official, had high ambitions for her son. His father, in contrast, wanted him to grow up to manage the family estates and live the life of a country squire. But in this case, the mother's wishes prevailed. Bismarck was sent to boarding school in Berlin at age six, and thereafter returned to his family home only on infrequent visits. His first school was one set up to train Prussian youth for high positions in the Army or the Court, and young Bismarck hated it.[1]

Continuing along the path laid out for him by his strong-minded mother, Bismarck finished this school, graduated from the best gymnasium, or high school, in Berlin, and entered law school at the prestigious University of Göttingen. Here he was a mediocre student, but with some tutoring he managed to pass the government entrance exams and was sent to Potsdam, then a small town outside Berlin, for his first assignment. But by this time he had become quite disillusioned with government service. He wrote to a cousin: "I find raising corn as respectable as writing administrative decrees and possibly more worthwhile. The Prussian civil servant is like the individual musician in an orchestra; he is confined to his own part which he plays as it is written, whether he likes it or not. I, however, want to make my own music in my own way or none at all."[2] Resigning his position in 1839, he returned to the country life he had not known since early childhood, taking over the lands he had inherited and managing to make them profitable despite a heavy burden of debt. He also gained a reputation for wildness. His neighbors called him "Mad Bismarck," a bachelor who would ride for miles across the countryside to go to parties and who would wear outlandish costumes on his occasional trips into town. He was also well known as a duelist, having fought a number of duels in his student days, and was often seen in the company of drinking companions and ladies of doubtful reputation.

Yet behind this eccentric and sometimes disreputable behavior, a sharp mind was at work. He once wrote: "History does not roll on like a railway train with even speed. It advances by fits and starts, but with irresistible force when it moves. One must be on the lookout and when one sees God striding through history, catch hold of His coattails and be dragged along as far as it may be."[3] In due course, Bismarck's choice of the life of a country squire, surrounded by adoring wife and children, dogs and horses, the homey rustic circle of his family, brought him full circle back into public life and gave him the opportunity that, in his view, God had provided.

FORGING A NATION

Bismarck's opportunity came in 1847, when he was elected to the Confederation Diet as the representative from his district in Prussia. At that time, the Diet was still nominally controlled by the Austrian Habsburg emperor in accordance with the terms of the Congress of Vienna. But the new delegate was determined to change this arrangement. Before long, he told his fellow delegates, "We shall have to fight for our lives against Austria; the march of events in Germany can have no other result."

Bismarck's physical appearance, along with his political methods, were key factors in his rise to leadership. He was a giant of a man, well over 6 feet (1.8 m) tall,

*An engraving of Otto von Bismarck,
from 1895, shows the Iron Chancellor
retaining his look of assurance and strength
even as he reached eighty.*

with deep-set eyes hooded like those of a hawk and a bristling mustache that made him the archetype of a Prussian officer even though he had little war experience. When he spoke, it was in a voice surprisingly soft and high-pitched, yet carrying absolute assurance in his message; listeners leaned forward in their seats in the Diet to catch every word.

His political methods are best described by the German word *Realpolitik*. One definition of it is "the politics of realism in which lack of principle is almost a matter of principle."[4] It might also be called a policy of expediency, taking into account the strengths and weaknesses of those involved in a conflict situation and playing on those strengths and weaknesses to one's own advantage. Realpolitik was not original to Bismarck, but he refined its use to such an extent that he is often considered its founder.

By 1862, Bismarck was in full stride behind God's coattails. Wilhelm I, the new Prussian king, appointed him chancellor—next to the ruler, the highest office in the Prussian state. Bismarck's "iron and blood" speech to the Diet excited the delegates; it seemed that the time was ripe for the Confederation to be transformed into a true German nation behind Prussia's leadership.

Chancellor Bismarck also gained the opportunity to stage-manage German foreign policy. His strategy was to use realpolitik to divide Germany's opponents and gain allies; this would forestall another European coalition against Prussia. His major foes were Austria and France. A century earlier, Austrian arms had nearly defeated Prussia. But Austria was now weaker militarily and territorially, largely due to the 1860 rebellion of the Italians, which had resulted in the formation of an independent Italy.

Prussia also held the edge in weapons. The Prussian chief of staff, Count Helmuth von Moltke (Bismarck's fellow Junker), had spent a couple of years in the United States observing the American Civil War, copying strategy and improvements in war equipment to build up Prussia's military strength. His men were also equipped with new rifles, developed by the German Krupp arms factory, that could be reloaded and fired six times as fast as those of the Austrians.

The final test came in 1866, near the village of König-grätz (now in the Czech Republic). Bismarck watched from the sidelines. A Prussian officer present at the battle wrote of him: "Mounted on a huge chestnut horse, wearing a great cloak, his great eyes gleaming, he reminded me of tales I had been told in childhood about giants of the frozen north."[5] It was a good omen; the Prussian "northerners" with their new assault rifles destroyed the Austrians, killing 10,000 in twenty minutes! The Habsburg empire survived, but only because Prussia did not press its advantage. Bismarck's goal was not territorial expansion but German unity.

THE SECOND REICH

The first German Reich, or realm, was the Holy Roman Empire of the German Nation, which was discussed in Chapter One. The Second Reich, formed in 1871 under Bismarck's prodding, was truer to the spirit of the German nation since it represented a confederation of contiguous and culturally similar German-speaking states. But despite Prussia's defeat of Austria and Bismarck's use of realpolitik to gain allies and disarm his European opponents, unity might still have eluded the Germans had there not been a change in Germany's relations with France, its ancient enemy and the last European power capable of preventing German unification.

French rulers had worked for years to keep Germany divided and weak, and after Napoleon's defeat they plotted revenge. On his part, Bismarck was convinced, and rightly so, that France would never allow the German states to unite; that would upset the balance of power in Europe. Here was a real test of realpolitik—how to provoke France into a declaration of war before its armies were fully prepared for combat. The Prussian Army was more than ready. It was battle-tested and had better equipment as well as the important military asset of mobility. The new rail lines built in western Germany in the 1840s and 1850s enabled German forces to be shifted quickly from one front to another, thus outflanking the French in their fixed fortress positions.

In 1870 a personal disagreement between Napoleon III—Bonaparte's nephew and since 1852 the emperor of France—and Wilhelm I escalated into conflict as Napoleon III declared war. Von Moltke's armies swept across the border into French territory and quickly outflanked French forces. The bulk of the French army was surrounded in the fortress city of Sedan on the Meuse River and forced to surrender. Napoleon III, who had accompanied the army in a vain attempt to rally his men, sat disconsolately in his carriage in an empty potato field until Bismarck came to greet him politely and take the French monarch into custody.

After the French surrender, the Prussian army then raced on to Paris, ringing the French capital with heavy artillery to back up its demand that France accept peace terms. With its armies in disarray and its ruler a war prisoner, the French government had little choice. Thus, on January 18, 1871, after peace had been declared, an unusual ceremony took place. King Wilhelm I of Prussia was crowned kaiser, or emperor, of the German nation, with Bismarck, in full-dress white uniform, and a bemedaled von Moltke beside him. What was noticeably unusual about the ceremony was that the crowning of a monarch of united Germany took place not on German soil but in the Hall of Mirrors of the Palace of Versailles,

An old illustration shows the
dramatic scene of Bismarck riding
forward to accept the surrender of
the defeated emperor, Napoleon III.

the traditional home of French monarchs. In effect, Bismarck was calling attention to the emergence of a new European power, one that would dominate European affairs during the next century and bring about profound changes in Europe and the world.

THE KAISERREICH

The new Germany's official name was the Kaiserreich, or "Realm of the Kaiser." Although it was weak economically and industrially in comparison with France and England, it was the largest unified state in central Europe. With the addition of Alsace-Lorraine, taken from France in 1870, German territory stretched from Metz in the west to Memel (modern Klaipeda, Lithuania) in the east. It was four-fifths the size of Texas, with a population in 1871 of 41 million. There was some industry and a good railway network, but most of the population was rural and followed a traditional way of life little changed over the years. Farming, fishing, and forestry were still the main occupations, and hard work, discipline, thrift, neatness, order, and obedience to authority were essential values.

The political structure of the Kaiserreich as formulated by Bismarck was that of a federal constitutional monarchy. There were three levels of government: the Kaiser, as head of state, with his chancellor and Cabinet of Ministers responsible for day-to-day operations; a Bundesrat (federal council) of representatives of the former German states and free cities, which advised the Kaiser and chancellor on policy matters; and a Reichstag (parliament) at the lowest level but, at least in theory, representing the people. Members of the Bundesrat were appointed by the chancellor, while the Reichstag was elected by direct male popular vote.

Germany's first parliamentary elections in history were held shortly after unification. Political parties had

In 1871 in the Palace of Versailles King Wilhelm I of Prussia was crowned kaiser of the German nation.

been legalized after 1848, and several participated. The National Liberal Party, a coalition of business, academic, and intellectual leaders, won a majority of seats. Whether the party could work with the authoritarian Iron Chancellor remained to be seen.

Unfortunately, a number of factors worked against the development of a democratic system in Germany. Bismarck was by nature antidemocratic; he was a conservative Prussian aristocrat in background and experience. The Kaiser was not really interested in taking an active part in government and left all policy decisions to Bismarck and the Bundesrat. This body was also dominated by Prussian Junker landowners, so much so that one observer called it "the constitutional fig-leaf of Prussian control over the Reich."[6] However, Wilhelm I, with his kindly blue eyes and long gray beard parted in the middle, helped to popularize the Prussian monarchy among all Germans by serving as a role model for what a good German, and particularly a good German monarch, ought to be—sober, virtuous, devoted to his family, a putterer in his garden, a ruler of simple tastes who preferred the country to the city.

ONE NATION, ONE GOVERNMENT

Having brought the German states into union, Bismarck's next task was to centralize the government. As with foreign policy, he applied realpolitik to domestic affairs, working in concert with Liberal Party leaders even though his instincts were authoritarian and elitist. A number of important laws were passed in the late 1800s to increase the powers of the central government. These laws set up a national court system and legal codes, a national bank (the Reichsbank), a single currency (the reichsmark), a postal system, and nationwide, government-run telephone and telegraph services.

His success in winning the cooperation of Liberal

Party leaders while simultaneously strengthening his own position augured well for a long future for the Iron Chancellor as Germany's effective head of state, especially as economic progress was bringing prosperity to more and more Germans. However, industrial development brought with it social problems. Motivated by the ideas of Karl Marx, a German-born economist, and his colleague Friedrich Engels, published in books such as *Das Kapital* and *The Communist Manifesto*, many working-class Germans began to challenge the idea that they lived in a rigid class structure in which one could never rise above one's family background and social status. Many intellectuals and academic leaders joined them in arguing that the stranglehold of the ruling class could be broken only through revolution. By the late 1880s, they had formed a new party, the Social Democrats, and were challenging the dominant Liberal Party for control of the Reichstag.

Despite his general support for social legislation, Bismarck was opposed to their plans to break up the traditional class structure and make Germany a democratic nation. In 1878 he forced a bill through the Reichstag that would outlaw "social democratic activities dangerous to the public welfare,"[7] but the language of the bill was vague and it proved difficult to enforce.

Matters came to a head when Kaiser Wilhelm I died in 1888, at the age of ninety-one. He had always agreed with Bismarck, and his support was important. His son and successor was already seriously ill and died three months later, his death bringing to the throne Wilhelm I's grandson Wilhelm, the Reich's third ruler in barely a year.

Wilhelm II was named for his grandfather, but the resemblance ended with the name. The new Kaiser had none of his grandfather's virtues and did not get along with Bismarck, who regarded him (as did many others) as a brash, incompetent upstart. On his side, Wilhelm II

Karl Marx, the German political philosopher, developed a theory of socialism that appealed to many working-class Germans and intellectuals frustrated by the restrictions of their society.

explained his plans in a private letter: "I'll just let the old man catch his breath for six months, then I'll rule by myself."[8]

As the last decade of the nineteenth century dawned, Kaiser Wilhelm II found himself with a situation he could use to get rid of Bismarck. Socialist representatives in the Reichstag had introduced new legislation that would give workers the right to strike, provide them with free education, health care, and legal services, and establish an eight-hour-a-day, five-day workweek. Germany today has the most extensive system of social benefits in the world, but in the 1890s such benefits as these seemed to Bismarck and his fellow government leaders as the first stage in the overthrow of the existing German political system of constitutional monarchy. Bismarck denounced the proposed legislation and said he would not accept it. But in this case realpolitik worked against him. The Kaiser, sensing an opportunity to get rid of "the old man," ordered him to formally present it for approval in accordance with his responsibilities under the constitution. But the Iron Chancellor stood firm. Refusing to compromise his principles, he retired from public life. With Bismarck gone, a safe, predictable era had ended and a new, unpredictable one had begun.

THE RISE
AND
FALL OF
EMPIRE

The King in Prussia—Forward;
Prussia in Germany—Forward;
Germany in the world—Forward!
—Bernhard von Bülow,
A Promise for Germany

At the dawn of the twentieth century, Germany was like a racehorse held back in its stable, an engine snorting and pawing the ground yet unsure of its direction. Prince Bernhard von Bülow, Bismarck's successor and, like him, a Junker aristocrat, spoke in these bold terms upon his accession to the office of chancellor. He and the Kaiser were kindred spirits, more so than the aging Bismarck could ever be to Wilhelm II, and the Kaiser's first address to his people echoed von Bülow's words but in the fine salty language of the accomplished yachtsman that he was: "I am now the officer on watch. The course remains the same. Full speed ahead!"[1]

Whether Wilhelm II's skills would serve Germany as well on land remained to be seen. He came to the job with a number of handicaps. He had been born with a withered arm, and though he kept it hidden under his coat when he went out in public, the deformity made him extremely self-conscious. His relationship with his own father had been poor, and he suffered all his life from low self-esteem, for which he often overcompensated with brash and opinionated statements. His poor self-image made him susceptible to flattery; he often did things without much thought and was most influenced by the last person who spoke with him, only to rush into some other rash action because of the influence of yet another speaker. He did have a good memory and grasp of technical ideas and welcomed new technology—especially in weapons, an area that fascinated him. Had he stayed out of the business of government and spent his time leading parades and handing out medals, he would probably be best remembered as the ruler who made monarchy popular with the German people, with its pomp and ceremony becoming as much a part of their lives as royalty is in England.

A CHANGING SOCIETY

The area where "full speed ahead" was the order of the day was the economy. Traditional German society consisted of two classes, the nobility and the peasants, with a small middle class of tradesmen, merchants, and artisans essential to village and town life. The wealth flowing in from economic growth helped create a new middle class of bankers, businessmen, and factory owners who challenged the power of the old nobility and made themselves influential in national life.

Industry began to grow at an extremely rapid rate in the late nineteenth century. The acquisition of Alsace-Lorraine, with its huge coal and iron resources, was a major factor in this growth. By 1900, Germany was producing more iron and steel than England, previously Europe's leading producer. Factories sprang up literally overnight in the Ruhr and other industrial areas, often with rows of dreary tenement buildings nearby to house the workers. The majority of these workers were illiterate peasants who migrated from rural farms or villages, their few possessions piled on top of hay wagons along with wives and children.

The growth of industry helped Germany to become Europe's leading producer and exporter of manufactured products in the early 1900s. Important companies such as Zeiss, Siemens, and Krupp (which are still in operation) became known throughout the world for their high-quality, precision-made products. As was the case in the United States, German banks and industries often joined in cartels, or syndicates, which made Germany a power in international finance. One German official during the period observed that the fate of the world was in the hands of 400 people, all of whom knew each other!

Another change in German society stemmed from the number of social benefits written into law by the Reichstag. A salaried lower middle class of clerks, cashiers, and others came into existence to administer these benefit programs. The members of this class wore white shirts with collars to work, were paid by the month, and felt themselves superior in every way to the factory workers in their blue shirts toiling away at their machines for an hourly or weekly wage. The new wealth benefited some members of the working class—highly skilled workers could now afford a bicycle, a daily shave at the barbershop, and a chicken on the table every Sunday at dinner. But most workers did not really share in the social improvements now available to the higher classes.

Despite this rapid industrialization and the extensive social changes that resulted from it, German society as a whole remained relatively static, preserving many of its old traditions and insulated from the political rivalries of the European powers or even the policies of their own government. An English traveler at the turn of the century has left us this delightful description of a typical German beer garden:

*. . . a troop of orderly, sober, decent, suave and
gentle persons of all ages and sexes were sitting at
little tables all covered with red-chequered table-cloths
and coffee-cups and glasses on them. Their children
sat beside them, and their dogs crouched at their feet
or circulated about the feet of other clients. Birds
hopped about under the tables, picking up crumbs
which these gentle people from time to time would
cast to them. There they sat, stolidly, composedly, as
if butter wouldn't melt in their mouths, gulping down
grosse Hellers and kleiner Dunklers, and more and
more of them. . . . Their dogs did not quarrel, the
birds still hopped about their toes in utter confidence;
everyone was sure that no chairs would be hurriedly
pushed in or angry words flout the sweet air they were
taking in, amid smoke of cigars or pipes, and the soft
breath of human converse. And discreet wives, with
their children of all ages to think about, kept an eye
on the sun and saw that it was declining. When they
thought it was time, they folded up their fancy work
. . . shook the crumbs off their children's bibs and
. . . turned their eyes westward to where the gilded
spires of Hildesheim seemed to point them to their
homes. Then men got up and shook themselves, and
paid.*[2]

As it was in the beer garden, so the tenor of German
country life remained constant in the years before the
Great Wars of 1914–1918 and 1939–1945. A resident
of Dachau, site of a notorious concentration camp in
World War II but an artists' colony in the 1890s, recalled:

*Those were halcyon days . . . when the sound of
whetstones on scythe blades filled the sultry late-
summer air, when painters roamed the moors and*

The traditional German beer garden

crowded the pubs, when the steam locomotive from Munich . . . could roll into the new Dachau train station, its whistle wailing, [while local characters lent spice to town life, like] the ironmonger who sang Wagner in his off hours, the town watchman, his sabre slapping his thigh and his leather helmet (with brass spike) on his head, who used to make the evening rounds and read [government] decrees from the steps of the Rathaus.[3]

FOREIGN POLICY—MARCH TO EMPIRE

Despite his ignorance of the outside world—he had traveled very little beyond Germany's borders—the Kaiser was determined to put his stamp on German foreign policy. His first goal was to make the Reich stronger militarily than any of its neighbors. This goal required the establishment of a powerful army and navy, the acquisition of colonies to provide the German economy with needed raw materials, and the conversion of industries to military production to develop improved weapons and equipment.

Germany was a late starter in the European game of acquiring colonies in Asia and Africa, and by 1900 most of the choice real estate was held by England or France. German colonies were established in Togo, the Cameroons, southwest Africa (now Namibia), and Tanganyika, all in Africa. Several small island groups in the South Pacific and the port of Tsingtao, on the Chinese mainland, completed the modest German colonial empire. As it turned out, these colonies were of little value to the German economy but were extremely important in international politics. Wishing to expand his trade into areas of Africa not yet controlled by the British or French, the Kaiser sent gunboats to the sultanate of Morocco on two occasions (1905 and 1911) to demand trading rights in that country. However, France disputed the claim and therefore worked out a secret deal with England for a French protectorate over Morocco. In return, England would receive a British protectorate over Egypt, thus leaving Germany out in the cold.

A similar situation developed when German engineers signed an agreement with the Ottoman Turkish sultan to build a railroad from Berlin to Baghdad. Today Baghdad is the capital of Iraq, but at that time it was a provincial capital of the Ottoman Empire. The Kaiser and his advisers hoped to strengthen Germany economically and politically by this project, outflanking the British Empire by a land march to the east (*Drang nach Osten*). But the railroad got only as far as Constantinople (Istanbul), the Ottoman capital, before British and French pressure caused it to be stopped.

The most unfortunate result of all these rivalries over land, power, and position was that it led the European powers closer and closer to a war that nobody really wanted. The Kaiser's ambition, paranoia, and susceptibility to flattery—and consequent rash decisions—had a great deal to do with the leaning toward war. He dreamed of a German Navy that would be equal in size and firepower to Britain's, and poured huge sums into shipbuilding. By 1913 the German Navy had fourteen "pocket" battleships, six cruisers, several packs of the deadly U-boats (submarines), and a fleet of torpedo-armed gunboats. The British countered with a naval buildup that included construction of several superbattleships called dreadnoughts. Other European powers were meanwhile building up their land forces. It would require only a tiny spark to set the fires of war alight.

A few farsighted leaders warned of the coming catastrophe. August Bebel, leader of the German Social Democrat Party, said prophetically in a 1911 speech: "Some fine day one side may say: Things cannot go on this

The Kaiser aimed to create a navy equal to that of the British, with packs of deadly submarines called U-boats, for untersee bootes. The British responded by building heavily armored battleships called dreadnoughts, after a famous ship of the Napoleonic wars.

way. . . . Then the catastrophe will unfurl. The general call to arms will resound across Europe, and 17 to 18 million men, the flower of their nations, armed with the most murderous of weapons, will march out to face one another on the field of battle. . . . What will be the result? . . . mass bankruptcy, mass misery, mass unemployment and mass starvation."[4]

The spark was lit with the assassination by a terrorist in 1914 of the Austrian crown prince, Franz Ferdinand, while he was visiting Sarajevo. This city, located in the formerly unified Republic of Yugoslavia, is today a battleground of Serbian, Bosnian, Christian, and Muslim groups fighting for control of that fragmented country. On the eve of World War I, it was part of the Austro-Hungarian empire, but its largely Serbian population (at that time) had been agitating for self-government as a first step to independence. Ferdinand's assassin was a member of the secret Serbian Black Hand terrorist organization, a group committed to independence through violent action. The assassination was intended to force the issue and prove that Austria could not control the area.

However, the assassination produced unforeseen results. Austria mobilized its army to take revenge on the rebellious Serbs. Russia, claiming its right to protect its fellow Slavs, declared war on Austria. A chain reaction followed as the Kaiser declared war on Russia on behalf of Germany's ally, Austria. The Ottoman sultan, allied with Germany since the abortive Berlin-Baghdad railway project, declared war on his old enemy, Russia. And France and England, Russia's allies, completed the circle by declaring war on Germany.

THE "WAR TO END ALL WARS"

World War I, as far as it affected Germany, was more of a European than a global war. As in 1871, German forces mobilized quickly and raced through neutral Belgium,

The unfortunate Archduke Franz Ferdinand
and his wife, Sophie Chotek, Duchess of
Hohenberg. Their assassination by a Serbian
nationalist is identified in history as
the immediate cause of World War I.

taking full advantage of surprise and superior firepower and mobility. They crossed the French border in August 1914, advancing as far as the Marne River east of Paris, where they stopped to regroup and wait for their slower artillery. On the eastern front, German armies raced across flatter terrain and trapped the main Russian army at Tannenberg, in East Prussia. But in neither case were the Germans able to follow up their initial advantage. French reinforcements rushed to the front in a fleet of ancient Paris taxis and halted the German advance at the Marne. In the east the Russians used the same tactics their great-grandfathers had used against Napoleon, trading territory for breathing space and drawing the Germans into marshes and forests. The war soon became a stalemate on both fronts. On the western front, French and British troops faced Germans, with deeply dug trenches on both sides and a "no-man's-land" of blood-soaked ground between them. The battles went on for days, weeks, months. Men lived underground like cave dwellers and lost all sense of time, concentrating upon the capture, or recapture, of a few hundred yards of territory. The casualties ran into the millions: an entire generation of Germans, Frenchmen, Britons, and others who were killed, wounded, or permanently crippled by poison gas. The Canadian poet John McCrae caught the spirit—and the tragedy—of the times in a famous poem:

In Flanders fields the poppies blow
Between the crosses, row on row.

Despite the stalemate on the war fronts, other factors began slowly to work against the Reich. The British fleet controlled the sea lanes; after one abortive attempt to engage the British that resulted in heavy losses, the German fleet, the Kaiser's pride and joy, stayed bottled up in the harbor. As a result, the British were able to impose

*Kaiser Wilhelm II (saluting) made
frequent visits to the battlefront,
but as the war went on, with huge
casualties mounting, he lost control
and popular support.*

a naval blockade on German ports. Food supplies ran low, and each time the government announced victories the people in the street muttered, *"Wir siegen uns zu tode!"* ("We will win victory right to the grave!"). The 1915–16 winter was especially hard on the German people. The only bread available was a loaf made of sawdust and bran,[5] the potato crop failed due to bad weather, and turnips were the staple vegetable. Those who survived called it the "turnip winter."

German commanders launched a submarine campaign in a desperate measure to break the blockade in 1915–17. Sleek, deadly U-boats armed with powerful torpedoes slipped out to sea like a pack of hungry sharks looking for kills. Their orders were to sink all ships bound for English ports, regardless of flag or country of origin. At first, shipping losses were heavy. But the campaign backfired when the Germans sank the Cunard (British) passenger liner *Lusitania* in the Atlantic. Among the more than 1,000 passengers aboard were 139 Americans. The loss aroused a storm of protest in the United States, leading to a declaration of war in 1917.

America's entry into the war was the final blow to German hopes. Thousands of American doughboys, bound for Europe and a date with "Kaiser Bill," embarked from New York before cheering crowds. A last-ditch offensive by the Germans, launched in an effort to reach Paris before the Americans arrived, failed. Just as in 1914, the Kaiser's forces were unable to exploit their initial advantage.

GERMANY SURRENDERS

In the end, the German people, not their leaders, gave up on a war that had become unwinnable. Sailors at the Wilhelmshaven naval base mutinied when the chief of staff, General Erich Ludendorff, ordered them out to sea to engage the British in one last battle. They took command of their ships and placed officers loyal to the general in irons. Factory workers in arms plants went on strike to stop production. In the Reichstag, speaker after speaker rose to demand that the Kaiser ask for peace talks based on the "Fourteen Points" speech of U.S. president Woodrow Wilson. A German general, Walther Reinhardt, wrote to his wife from the front: "We must admit reality. Over a million men have sacrificed their lives for the . . . Fatherland. . . . A struggle solely for the sake of honour can be probably demanded of a good army unit, but . . . not of an entire people."[6]

Pressured on all sides, the Kaiser was persuaded to abdicate and fled secretly to exile on a farm in nearby Holland. Ludendorff sought sanctuary in neutral Sweden behind dark glasses and a false Swedish name. In Berlin the leader of the Social Democrats declared Germany a republic. It was a bold move, especially with the bitter taste of defeat on everyone's lips.

THE WEIMAR REPUBLIC

Germany's surrender and the Kaiser's abdication left the country without an effective government. An armistice was signed on November 11, 1918, to end the fighting, but who could form a government acceptable to the victors and also negotiate peace terms? Only the Reichstag remained as a viable political institution, and it was the Reichstag that took action. The Social Democrat leader, Philipp Scheidemann, was eating his lunch, a bowl of potato soup, in his office when a huge crowd surrounded the parliament building. Radical speakers with bullhorns harangued the crowd, demanding "peace, bread and freedom," words that had preceded the Communist Revolution and overthrow of the czar in Russia in 1917. It seemed that a workers' state was about to emerge in Germany. Scheidemann was fiercely opposed to Communism. A bold gamble seemed necessary to block its progress. He jumped up, ran to his office window, opened it, and leaned out shouting, "The government has resigned! The Kaiserreich is no more! Germany is a republic!"[7] Then he closed the window and returned to his soup.

Rarely in history has such a radical change in government taken place in such an offhand fashion. But Scheidemann's move worked. Socialist leaders and other prominent officials supported him. The Reichstag was called into emergency session and approved a constitution to establish a republic in Germany. Another Socialist leader and Reichstag deputy, Friedrich Ebert, was elected as its first president.

However, Germany's first experiment in democracy faced serious problems from the beginning. The problems were both political and economic. The capital was moved from Berlin to Weimar, a quiet town associated with the best in German culture (Goethe, Schiller, and other writers, composers, and artists had lived and worked there), in an effort to erase the memories of defeat associated with the Kaiser's regime. But many Germans felt uncomfortable with a republican system. They were used to authoritarian, patriarchal leadership and preferred a "father figure" who would make decisions for them and deal with looming postwar problems. Others argued for a Communist regime that would redistribute national wealth and give political power to workers. Still others, many of them discharged war veterans, were convinced that government leaders had let them down, that Germany had not lost the war but had been betrayed. This "stab in the back" theory was widespread and led to the rise of a Freikorps (Free Corps) of right-wing nationalists dedicated to the overthrow of the republic and the establishment of a military dictatorship.

One of the points made by Woodrow Wilson in his "Fourteen Points" speech to the U.S. Senate called for fair peace terms for Germany. But when the Weimar

With throngs of observers in attendance,
delegates of Germany and the allied
nations signed a peace treaty in the Hall
of Mirrors of the Palace of Versailles.

Republic's representatives met those of the victorious Allies in the same Hall of Mirrors at Versailles where the Second Reich had been launched fifty years earlier, the atmosphere was very different. Each of the victors had a different agenda. France wanted to make sure that Germany would never again be a threat. Britain's prime minister had promised his people that the Reich would pay dearly for the war. Italy sought to recover lost territory at Austria's expense. Wilson's dream of a fair peace was buried under a tangled mat of European power politics. Unlike the Congress of Vienna, which had restored the balance of power and allowed a defeated France to take part in the discussions, the victors simply dictated peace terms to a defeated Germany.

The other major problem for the republic was the heavy burden of war reparations, imposed at the same time that left- and right-wing groups, Communists, war veterans, and many others were struggling for the right to control the government and shape the "new" Germany of the future. The reparations burden accelerated economic collapse. By 1923 the German mark was worthless; it took 4.2 *trillion* marks to make a dollar. This disaster not only wiped out people's savings; it also destroyed their faith in an ordered and predictable world. Prices rose astronomically. A survivor of the time recalled: ". . . our classmates had to leave the gymnasium [high school] because their parents couldn't finance it any longer. . . . A bread roll cost 20 million marks, a quart of milk 300 million marks."[8] Helped by foreign (mostly United States) aid, the economy improved in the late 1920s, only to fall apart again with the stock market crash of 1929 and the worldwide Great Depression that followed.

It can be argued that the Weimar Republic's survival for fourteen years (1919–1933) against such odds was a measure of success. Indeed, its constitution included a bill of rights with special provisions to protect the sanctity of marriage and the needs of the working classes. Voting rights were given to women, the Reichstag became the center of political and legislative power, and the election system was changed to one of proportional representation rather than the simple majority system of the Kaiserreich. Also, the efforts of leaders like Gustav Stresemann to solve economic problems and cooperate with leaders of other European nations led to Germany's acceptance by the international community as a peace-loving state. The Dawes Plan, named for American banker Charles G. Dawes, set up a regular payment schedule for war debts; in return, Germany became eligible for foreign loans to help revive the economy and thus guarantee debt repayments. Foreign capital, mostly from American banks, began to flow into the country.

Stresemann also worked to improve Germany's relations with its neighbors. The Locarno Treaties, signed in Locarno, Switzerland, with France, Belgium, and Holland, fixed the country's western borders except for Alsace-Lorraine, returned to France with the peace treaty. French troops left the Ruhr, and in 1926 Germany was accepted as a member of the League of Nations. In 1928, along with fifteen other nations, Germany signed the U.S.-sponsored Kellogg-Briand Pact outlawing war as an instrument of national policy.

Internal instability rather than outside pressures or even economic problems eventually led to the downfall of the Weimar Republic. The Spartacus League, an extreme left-wing group, tried in 1919–20 to set up a Soviet-style workers' state, but the attempt was crushed by loyal army units aided by the Freikorps—these extreme-right-wing war veterans hated Communism more than they hated democratic government. In Bavaria, which had a Catholic majority and had been the last German state to join the Second Reich, leaders spoke openly of union with Catholic, German-speaking Austria next door. Weimar

Gustav Stresemann (center), seen at a reception of foreign journalists in Berlin, worked to reconcile the former World War I adversaries and to restore Germany's international status. He was awarded a Nobel Peace Prize in 1926.

government officials were attacked, and several of them murdered, by Freikorps "hit squads"; right-wing nationalist leaders accused those officials of being "November criminals" (responsible for the 1918 armistice) or "appeasement politicians" who had engineered Germany's defeat in the war.

Under such circumstances it was probably inevitable that a new authority figure, perhaps another Hermann or Frederick the Great or Bismarck, would appear to take charge of German destinies. The sudden collapse of monarchy had left nothing in its place; the German people had no experience with the process of the accommodation of competing interests that makes democracy possible. Shortly before his death in 1929, Gustav Stresemann wrote prophetically: "The future now lies in the hands of the young generation, the youth of Germany whom we could have won over to peace and the new Europe. I fear both have been lost—if so, that is my tragedy." The failure of the republic, while it was his tragedy, was not his fault. He and his associates had come out of the ordered, stable world of Bismarck's Second Reich. That world had come apart in the Great War, and in its aftermath they were caught up in the whirl of social and economic, as well as political, reform; without the power to carry through with needed changes or provide the leadership that would make their new world work. The alternative was National Socialism, with its crude yet powerful message, articulated by a speaker who could rouse a crowd to fever pitch and carry them unthinkingly toward his negative and destructive goals.

FIVE

THE
THIRD REICH

Heute gehoert uns Deutschland,
Morgen die Ganze Welt.
(Today we rule Germany,
Tomorrow the whole world.)
—From the Storm
Troopers' anthem

In later years it would become a terrifying battle cry, launched hoarse-voiced from thousands of throats of brown-shirted troopers as they marched past Adolf Hitler in the heady early days of the Third Reich. But in 1919–20 National Socialism had no anthem, no symbol to attract interest. It was one of many ideas taken up by groups in the Weimar Republic. More nationalist than Socialist, it appealed mainly to working people, ordinary people who met in beer gardens to talk about Germany's problems over foaming mugs of lager. These problems, they argued, were caused by Jews, Communists, bankers, capitalists—anyone who was different from them and therefore supposedly exploited the working classes. With the establishment of the Weimar Republic, they moved toward political action, and in 1919 four men—a machinist, a newspaperman, a dentist, and a railroad worker—organized the German Workers' Party (DAP). The founders had been members of the Thule Society, a racist, anti-Semitic society similar in certain respects to the Ku Klux Klan in the United States. The society's logo and symbol was the swastika.[1]

The DAP was very small, averaging ten to forty members at its weekly meetings. But despite its size, its opposition to the Versailles Treaty and the Weimar government that signed that treaty, gave it two advantages over larger and more visible groups like the Communists. First, its headquarters was in Munich, Bavaria, traditional center of opposition to rule from Berlin and the Protestant north. Second, although the ideas of National Socialism and particularly its antidemocratic, anticapitalist, anti-Semitic stand, as well as its refusal to accept German war guilt, were not generally accepted by the German people, many Germans privately agreed with them. Theodor Heuss, who later became the first president of the German Federal Republic, once observed that National Socialism was not born in Munich but at Versailles, and certainly one of its major drawing cards was its rejection of the humiliating terms of the peace treaty.

Despite these advantages, the DAP's prospects for political success were at best poor. Then, on September 12, 1919, it seemed as if God had intervened to bring its members a leader. A stranger joined their meeting and listened quietly, but when the talk turned to the possibilities of a union of Catholic Bavaria with Catholic Austria he jumped up and denounced the idea so loudly and angrily that someone whispered, "Man he has a big mouth; we could use him."[2] As the stranger was leaving, someone noted down his name and address, and sometime later he received a card for membership in the German Workers' Party. The card bore the name Adolf Hitler.

Today, the very name Hitler is a symbol for a ruthless tyrant, a dictator, an oppressor, a megalomaniac. But the stranger who wandered into the Munich beer hall meeting of the German Workers' Party almost three quarters of a century ago was not only unknown to the members and the world at large; he was not even of German birth.

Hitler's father's family name was Schicklgruber; the family came from a small village in Austria, not far from the German border. His father, Alois, had had his name legally changed to Hitler (alternately Hiedler or Hüttler), which was that of his stepfather. (To this day, nothing is known about Hitler's grandfather or his paternal ancestry.) Alois Hitler was a self-made man who had risen from poor origins to a high position in the Austrian customs service. He was fifty-two when Adolf was born, in 1889, and dominated his wife and family so completely that she always called him "uncle" (she was actually his niece). He was a harsh and authoritarian father; Hitler's sister Paula recalled that as a child "Adolf got his sound thrashing every day."[3]

Thus we see in Hitler's childhood several formative influences: uncertainty about his family background, a poor relationship with his father, and kindness but little guidance or protection from his timid mother.

Alois Hitler had hoped that his son would finish school and enter the Austrian customs service like himself. But young Adolf had other ideas: he dreamed of becoming an artist, but not only to oppose his father. The goal also resulted from the fantasy world he had built in order to escape from the daily drudgery and misery of his home life and such failures as his inability to make friends and his poor performance in school (he never finished high school).

The opportunity to pursue his dream came unexpectedly after his father's sudden death, of a cerebral hemorrhage, while drinking beer in a local tavern. His mother was unable to function without her husband and died soon afterward, leaving Hitler a small inheritance. Hitler then moved to Vienna, the Austrian capital and one of Europe's most important centers of music, art, and literature. He believed that here at last he could follow an artistic career.

However, success continued to elude Hitler in Vienna. His application to attend the famous Academy of Fine Arts was turned down; the drawings he submitted were judged of poor quality and more suited to architecture than art. Yet when he applied for admission to the Vienna architecture school, his application was also rejected because he had not finished high school. Fortunately, his inheritance was enough for him to live comfortably for a time, and he spent his days sketching buildings, reading in libraries, and standing at the back of the Vienna Opera House to hear performances of his favorite operas, particularly those of Wagner. When his money ran out, he drew watercolor postcards to sell to tourists and slept on park benches or in shelters for the homeless.

During his time in Vienna, Hitler also developed his obsessive hatred of Jews. Anti-Semitism, the fear and dislike of Jews, did not originate with Hitler; it goes back to Roman times 2,000 or more years ago and is deeply embedded in European culture. Ever since Christianity became the dominant religion of the Roman Empire and was passed on to its European successor states, Christian dogma has been hostile to Jews. Jews were accused of killing Christ, an act actually committed by the Romans. Also, Jews in Europe were disliked because they refused to abandon their religion and accept Christ as the Messiah.

Jews in non-Christian areas such as the Islamic lands of Africa and the Middle East and Islamic Spain during the Middle Ages were infrequently persecuted as a group and took part in Islamic life as a protected community. Anti-Semitism in Europe also varied from country to country and period to period in history. In Germany, for example, thousands of Jews were killed, robbed, or forced

The great German composer
Richard Wagner whose works
were revered by Hitler

to convert to Christianity during the period of the Crusades, a series of military campaigns organized by the Catholic Church to recover the holy city of Jerusalem from hostile Islamic control.

Another wave of persecutions followed the Protestant Reformation. Martin Luther had encouraged Jews to convert to Christianity, arguing that when the Protestants had purged the religion of its Catholic elements and made it pure again, it would attract Jewish converts. But when the Jews did not respond, he turned against them, calling them usurers, parasites, devils, or worse, and urging people to burn their synagogues and destroy their sacred books. Luther's hatred of Jews was to be a tragic part of his legacy to future generations of Germans.

After Luther, and particularly in the eighteenth and nineteenth centuries, when religious tolerance increased and the Industrial Revolution brought great social changes to Europe, Jews gradually moved into the mainstream of European life. Their skills, intelligence, and commitment to education enabled many of them to do well as bankers, lawyers, and doctors. Other Jews prospered as jewelers and owners of neighborhood grocery shops and other stores providing essential services to their communities.

Yet this almost subliminal anti-Semitism has persisted through the centuries. A German who had worked for a Jewish jeweler in Munich for forty years and was confronted with the anti-Jewish behavior loose in Hitler's Third Reich mused: "He had never thought of the Silvers as Jews so that it embarrassed him to be reminded of it because it roused certain unconscious, negative feelings about Jews in general, feelings that had survived intact precisely because he did not think of the Silvers as Jews."[4]

In the late nineteenth century, anti-Semitism was given a new impetus by German philosophers like Fichte and Hegel. They argued that the Germans were racially and culturally superior to all other peoples and were therefore tainted by the presence of Jews in their midst. Wilhelm Marr, a respected German scholar, took the argument a step farther when he wrote a book criticizing Jews for their control of German economic life. Marr's views and those of a pro-German English writer, Houston Chamberlain, who glorified German culture and denounced Jews as a "negative race" lacking a true religion, also influenced Hitler in his obsessive conviction that Jews more than any other group were responsible for Germany's postwar problems.

But Hitler's violent anti-Semitism lay in the future. World War I was the first great turning point in his life. He had left Vienna in 1913 and emigrated to Munich, possibly to avoid being drafted into the Austrian Army but more probably to fulfill his desire to become fully German. When war broke out, he volunteered for a German regiment and spent the entire war at the front. By all accounts he was a brave soldier. He was wounded twice, promoted to corporal on the battlefield, and received the Iron Cross, First Class, Germany's highest military decoration, for bravery under fire.

While recovering from the second round of wounds in a Berlin hospital, Hitler received the bitter news of Germany's surrender and the flight of the Kaiser. Like many other demoralized veterans in search of easy answers, he jumped to the conclusion that the war had been lost not by the men at the front but by weak leaders and Jewish bankers at home. He decided then that his real purpose in life was to seek revenge on those who had betrayed Germany, and a mission to enter politics replaced his hopeless dream of becoming an artist.

His opportunity came with the unexpected invitation to join the German Workers' Party. He decided to attend its next meeting and found a handful of people hunched over a gas lamp, sitting around a battered table in the back room of a run-down tavern. The minutes of the

Hitler believed that the German soldiers
who had suffered through the war years,
fighting and dying in battlefield
foxholes, had been betrayed.

previous meeting were read, and the party treasurer reported cash on hand as seven marks fifty pfennigs. It was not a promising start for a party whose stated goals were to abolish capitalism and overthrow the Weimar Republic. But to Hitler, destiny seemed to be beckoning. He asked a few questions and then abruptly accepted the membership invitation. He was issued membership card number 555, but he was actually the fifty-fifth member, the membership roll having started with number 500 to make the party appear larger than it actually was.

Remembering his big mouth, the members put him in charge of recruitment and propaganda. It was a good choice. Having no job, Hitler could devote all his time to party activities. But his greatest value to the DAP was his speaking ability. Hitler's speeches had a hypnotic effect on his audiences. He would stand stiffly erect, stray locks of hair falling across his domed forehead, head thrown slightly backward, right arm raised with index finger rhythmically stabbing the air to emphasize his words, voice rising steadily to a high falsetto as he shouted until he was almost hoarse.[5] His Monday night sessions at the Café Neumann became the highlight of Munich social life, and as a result party membership grew rapidly.

Another source of public support for the DAP came from its change of name, as suggested by Hitler. The new name was the National Socialist German Workers' Party (Nationalsozialistische Deutsche Arbeiterpartei, commonly shortened to "Nazi"). Hitler argued that the new name would appeal to all segments of the population—it was "national," "socialist," and worker oriented. Party meetings and parades now featured the Nazi flag, a blood-red banner with a black swastika in a white circle in its center—red for Socialism, white for the nation, black for the pure Aryan German nation, a concept borrowed by the Nazis from Fichte, Chamberlain, and other influential writers.

Hitler's oratory and force of personality soon made him the Nazi Party's leader. German culture has always featured a *Führer*, or leader, a father figure who appears to take charge of the nation in times of trouble and whom the people follow with blind obedience because they believe he will lead them to greatness. As early as 1922, an article in a Munich newspaper called Hitler "the great man of deed, the fearless leader of Germany's resurrection."[6] Party members looked up to him as the leader sent to them by destiny to free Germany from the shackles of Versailles and make it a great power again.

As the party's membership grew, ideas and symbols from other groups and even other societies were borrowed to cultivate the Nazi image. The Nazi slogan *"Ein Volk, Ein Reich, Ein Führer"* ("One People, One State, One Leader") was borrowed from the Fascist Party, then in power in Italy; as were the brown shirts that became the Nazi uniform and the outstretched "Heil Hitler" right arm salute, palm downward (which was also the Nazi answer to the Communist clenched-fist salute). These symbols helped mold an organization unthinkingly dedicated to Hitler's goal of a racially pure German society, a *Herrenvolk* ("master race") with non-Germans excluded. In keeping with this exclusive society, the old idea of *Lebensraum* ("living space") was redefined by the Nazis to give the Germans the right to take over the lands of so-called racially and culturally "inferior" peoples. This would provide room for Germany to expand.

By 1923 the party had 6,000 members in Munich alone, with branches throughout Germany and as far away as Vienna. Its treasury had increased enormously, not only from dues but also from the contributions of Bavarian businessmen and industrialists who disliked the Weimar government's Socialist policies. The Nazis had also organized their own military force, the Storm Troopers (Sturmabteilung, or SA). It began as "a motley rabble of 2,000 unemployed roughnecks," according to Nazi leader Hermann Göring.[7] The SA's job was to protect party meetings and disrupt those of its rivals, but before long, under the leadership of Göring and a scar-faced ex-army captain, Ernst Röhm, the Storm Troopers ruled the streets of Munich, "brawling their way to greatness," as they put it in their marching songs. In their gray ski caps, brown shirts, windbreakers with swastika armbands, and knobby walking sticks, they were indeed a feared group, loyal to no authority except that of Hitler and their own leaders.

Encouraged by local leaders in Munich, Hitler organized a march on Berlin in November 1923. He was confident that the German people would join the Nazis in overthrowing the inept Weimar government. But the "Beer Hall Putsch," so called because it began in Munich's largest beer hall, never got out of the city. Police and reinforced army units met the marchers with a hail of gunfire; fourteen Nazis were killed, and Hitler was arrested and charged with high treason.

Ironically, this failure proved to be a turning point in Hitler's career. He was sentenced to a five-year jail term, the maximum allowable under the law, and was released for good behavior after serving nine months of his sentence. During his time in prison, he wrote *Mein Kampf* ("My Struggle"), his autobiography and the "bible" of the Nazi Party. Most of it was dictated to his bodyguard Emil Maurice, a burly ex-thug, and to Rudolf Hess, an early Nazi whose loyalty to Hitler was such that he volunteered to serve time in prison with his leader.[8]

Their failure also forced the Nazis to work within the political system, much as they despised it, in order to gain power. Joseph Goebbels, a journalist and unsuccessful novelist, joined the party in 1925 and quickly became its chief propaganda spokesman. Goebbels's use of the "Big Lie," placing posters with slogans such as "He who thinks German must despise the Jews" and "Communism is the Death of Germany" in public places, reached the sense

Two posters supporting the Social
Democrats in the 1930 general elections
demonstrate the political turmoil of the
period. The top one can be translated as,
"The one who votes for the Communists
frees the political assassins." The lower
poster can be read as: "We won't stand for
this. We're voting Social Democrat."

of deep anger and frustration even among people who did not care for the Nazis and disapproved of their methods.[9]

Germany's economic difficulties also played into Nazi hands, especially after the Great Depression had eliminated the gains of Stresemann's program. In the 1930 elections to the Reichstag, to everyone's surprise "107 rowdy brown-shirted Nazis took their seats before a stunned crowd."[10] In the 1932 elections, the party doubled its representation. Its next move was to nominate Hitler for president against the incumbent, Hindenburg, who was in line for a second term. The Nazi leader lost in a close vote, but his public support was such that it seemed only a matter of time before the Nazis would come to power.

And indeed, on a gloomy January day in 1933, destiny enfolded Adolf Hitler in its coattails. Leaders of the Weimar government advised President Hindenburg to name Hitler reichschancellor. No one else had public confidence any longer, they warned. Hindenburg was still not convinced. "This man is Austrian," he said. "He is up to no good. You want me to hand over power to this small-town gangster?" In reality, Hindenburg had no choice. The alternatives had been tried and had failed. Hindenburg called Hitler into the conference room (he had been waiting in an outer office, practicing his bows and smiles before a hall mirror) and without so much as a greeting appointed him reichschancellor. The two men then went out onto the balcony of the government palace overlooking Wilhelmstrasse, the broad avenue named for Kaiser Wilhelm I. Below them, thousands of storm troopers and party members with flaming torches marched past carrying the swastika banner of Nazism. In the Opera House nearby, the curtain rose on a performance of Wagner's *Götterdämmerung*, Hitler's favorite opera in his long-ago Vienna days. It seemed a fitting start for the Third Reich.

SIX

THE
NAZI IMPACT

Just as Adolf Hitler has raised
the German people to new life
in heroic struggle, we find in his
own life the eternal rebirth of
the German nation.

—Otto Dietrich,
*Eulogy on Hitler's
Birthday* (1935)

Well before they came to power, the Nazis had predicted
a thousand-year life span for the Third Reich. Once they
had won control of the government, they moved swiftly
to lay the foundations of lasting existence. The first stage
was the elimination of rival political parties, notably the
Communists and Socialists, who between them held a
majority of seats in the Reichstag. Goebbels warned: "We
shall observe all the niceties of the law in order to get
power, but we shall use it the moment we have it."[1]
That moment came one night in February 1933, barely a
month after Hitler had been named reichschancellor,
when the Reichstag building in Berlin was set on fire and
burned to the ground. A Dutch member of the German
Communist Party was caught leaving the scene and con-
fessed to the crime. Although the evidence was circum-

stantial—many scholars today believe the Nazis set the fire themselves and used the Dutchman as a scapegoat— Hitler declared that the arson offered clear proof of a Communist plot to set up a Soviet-style state in Germany. He persuaded the aging Hindenburg to grant him emergency powers to deal with the situation. Hindenburg was ill and died the following year; he was not to live to see the republic he had led in its last years turned into a Nazi Reich. But even as Hindenburg lay on his deathbed, Hitler moved to make himself absolute master of Germany. The emergency powers given Hitler suspended civil and constitutional rights. The Communist Party was declared illegal, and several thousand members were arrested and packed off to detention camps set up in abandoned factories or isolated rural areas. A similar treatment was meted out to Socialists who spoke out against the violation of people's rights.

With political opposition neutralized, Hitler could implement his plans to make himself absolute master of the Reich. The Reichstag voted to combine the offices of president and reichschancellor into one office. Hitler was now Führer of all the Germans, an incredible leap upward in a decade and a half for the fifty-fifth member of a ragtag workers' party.

The only potential opposition to Hitler's authority lay within his own party—in the Storm Troopers. They were larger in numbers than the regular German Army, which was still limited to 100,000 men under the Versailles Treaty. Their leader, scar-faced Captain Ernst Röhm, had built them into a brawling but powerful fighting force, more loyal to him than to Hitler. Röhm talked openly of a "second Nazi revolution" that would bring the regular army under Storm Trooper control, making the Storm Troopers the most powerful force in the country. Röhm's rivals warned Hitler that he was dangerous and that he planned a coup. At first, the Führer did not believe them, but when evidence was produced he was convinced. In June 1934, units of Hitler's special body-guard, the Schutzstaffel ("Security Units," or SS) sur-rounded Storm Trooper barracks and offices and arrested Röhm and other leaders. The so-called "Night of the Long Knives" followed as they were executed without trial. In a radio address, Hitler justified the executions as necessary because of the danger to the nation. "We acted in self-defense," he said. Not surprisingly, the majority of the German people accepted his explanation; as would happen throughout the Nazi period, loyalty and obedi-ence to an authority figure overrode their dislike of extra-legal methods.

ECONOMIC PROGRESS

The economy was one of the few areas of national life that benefited under the Nazi regime. Hitler had drawn up an economic program for the party's original platform in 1920, and to his credit he left economic development mainly in the hands of experts, while introducing new programs intended to benefit the working classes. A Win-ter Aid program designed to help the elderly, especially widows and pensioners, provided health care, housing, food, and other services to these "poorest of the poor"; it seemed to many of them a gift from heaven by way of their Führer.[2] The regime also undertook huge public works programs to provide thousands of new jobs. Ger-mans worked shoulder to shoulder to build the *autobahnen* (highways), enormous public buildings, and other struc-tures associated with the "bigness" of the Nazi period. Universal labor service plus military conscription all but eliminated unemployment; young people who could not find their own jobs could enter either the army or the labor corps.

German industry also gained significantly under the Third Reich. Until the country was put on an arms production footing as war loomed in the late 1930s, German factories were not interfered with; the Nazis needed the financial and moral support of industrial leaders. As a result, production of civilian goods and exports soared. International successes such as the first nonstop transatlantic flight of a lighter-than-air dirigible (the *Graf Zeppelin*) and the fastest transatlantic crossing by a passenger liner, also German, boosted German pride and confidence in German workmanship.

THE NAZIFICATION OF GERMAN LIFE

It was in the area of social and cultural life that the Nazi hand fell heaviest. It may seem strange that a society that has contributed so much to world civilization over the centuries in music, art, literature, and drama, a society of humanists and philosophers, would fall prey to the sterile, unimaginative ideology of Nazism. One possible explanation was suggested by Otto Kumm, a printer who joined the Nazis in 1930. He said: "One could try a new beginning with the Communists, or join the National Socialists who were working to free the country from the stranglehold of the Versailles Treaty and make it independent once again. I couldn't see any third option back then, and I guess millions of other Germans couldn't either."[3] The innate German tradition of obedience and order, along with Hitler's charismatic leadership, certainly made the Nazis' task easier. Theirs was to be a purification of Germany from all foreign influences and particularly decadent (which usually meant Jewish) ones.

One element in Nazification was the glorification of Hitler. The Führer's birthday, April 20, was declared a national holiday. Speakers vied for his favor with lengthy eulogies, and families planted "Hitler oaks" in their yards as if to link the leader with the forested German past, with national heroes like Hermann. Although many

Germans still preferred the traditional "*Grüss Gott*" as their greeting, the "*Heil Hitler*" salute was mandated by decree and soon became the standard form.[4]

Hitler especially detested twentieth-century "modern" art, with its emphasis on freedom of expression and experimentation with new techniques. In 1937 the Nazis held an exhibit of what they called "Degenerate Art," featuring works by Klee, Kandinsky, Picasso, and other modern masters. The exhibit was held in a badly lit room, with vulgar jokes and graffiti scrawled under the paintings. Hitler said it would prove that the only "true" art of the day was being created by pure (non-Jewish German) traditional artists.[5]

To achieve their goal to create a generation of young Germans fully indoctrinated in Nazism, the Nazis set out to purge the educational system. They took complete control of the press and other media. Teachers and professors who were either Jewish or were not party members lost their positions, as did journalists, editors, and reporters. Newspapers and magazines were regularly censored, while books by Jewish authors or by writers deemed unsympathetic to Nazi ideology were removed from libraries and burned in huge bonfires. The German people were also deprived of their greatest cultural asset, their intellectual leaders, when most of Germany's best scientists, philosophers, artists, and intellectuals fled the country. Many emigrated to Britain, France, or the United States, enriching the cultural life of their new countries immeasurably.

The number-one priority of the party in its Nazification program was the indoctrination of youth. The subjects stressed in the school curriculum—German history (presented in National Socialist terms), biology (to explain Nazi racist ideology), and the German language—ensured the production of unthinking little Nazis. Boys were specially trained; Hitler said he wanted his young

The standard-bearers of the SA corps
lead a Nazi march through the streets
of Nuremberg in 1933.

men to be "quick as greyhounds, tough as leather, and hard as Krupp steel."[6] Membership in the Hitlerjugend (Hitler Youth) was mandatory for those who wished to advance in the Nazi Party.

HITLER ATTACKS THE JEWS

The Führer's lifelong hostility toward the Jews formed the core of his plan to remake German society along pure racial lines. However, the Jewish community in Germany seemed not to have recognized the danger of his particular brand of anti-Semitism. One reason was that Jews had become well established in many professions and were integrated into society; they spoke German and often could not be distinguished from their German Christian counterparts. Jews were well represented in the legal profession, in medicine, and in banking, and Jewish grocers and shopkeepers were essential to many German neighborhoods. When Goebbels railed against "the poor Jew next door, whose cousin is the rich capitalist bent on world domination,"[7] most Jews and many of their German neighbors dismissed the statement as empty propaganda.

Thus the attack on the Jews as a community seemed to come without warning. The first step was a boycott of all Jewish-owned shops and businesses. Storm troopers roamed city streets beating up elderly Jews, and signs— "The good German does not buy from a Jewish shop"— were nailed up at the entrances to Jewish-owned establishments. The boycott was called off after three days, largely due to protests from abroad, but the damage had been done. Jews in Germany would never feel the same again.

A series of new laws depriving Jews of their constitutional rights were passed next, to encourage them to emigrate. A Jew was defined as anyone with one or more Jewish grandparents. No one in this category could hold

Crowds greet a Hitler Youth march
with fascist salutes.

a government job, teach in schools or universities, or serve in the armed forces. Jewish children were excluded from the public schools. Jews could not own land and were prohibited from using public facilities such as swimming pools and movie theaters under the Nuremberg Laws (so called because they were devised in the city of Nuremberg, later the site of the important war crimes trials of Nazi leaders after World War II).[8] Jews were issued special ID cards and ordered to add "Israel" or "Sarah" to their names to show their racial status. Some towns even posted signs saying "No Jews Allowed" at the town limits.

On November 9, 1938, anti-Jewish violence reached its peak. A German diplomat in Paris had been shot by a teenage Jewish refugee, and Hitler used the incident as a pretext to send out his SS "goons" on a mission of destruction. SS units and storm troopers went on a rampage, smashing, burning, and looting Jewish-owned shops, homes, and synagogues all over Germany. When it was over, the death toll of Jews stood at 91, and for the first time the entire Jewish community was affected as more than 30,000 Jews were arrested and held in detention. They were released only upon payment of a large fine levied on the entire Jewish community. The violence horrified many non-Jewish Germans, and in some cities, notably Leipzig and Baden-Baden, citizens protested. But other gentile Germans joined in with the perpetrators. In one town, women and children helped SS units destroy the town synagogue. The date of November 9 is preserved in Jewish memory as Kristallnacht, the "Night of Broken Glass," named for the shards of broken glass that littered city streets for days thereafter and which Jews were ordered to clean up, while the Nazis charged that the Jews had interfered with Germany's economic progress.

From Kristallnacht on, Jews were no longer considered citizens of the Reich. They were "Jewish workers" with a status similar to that of the foreign workers (*Gastarbeiters*) in Germany today. As a result, Jewish emigration increased rapidly; by 1939, 40 percent of Germany's Jewish population had fled the country.

THE OPPOSITION

Although the "cult of Hitler" and the persuasiveness of Nazi ideology, along with the popularity of the party's campaign to make Germany a great power again, made Nazism acceptable to the majority of the German people, here and there courageous individuals spoke out against the regime. The Communist Party had been outlawed, but some members went underground and served as agents of the Soviet Union, keeping the Soviet government informed about German arms production and military plans. After Kristallnacht, some Christian families in Germany hid Jews in their homes or helped them escape from the country, often at great personal risk.

In some parts of Germany there was even political opposition; one town in the Erzgebirge, a chain of hills in the Sudetenland along what later became the border of East Germany, voted solidly Social Democratic as late as 1938.[9] There was also considerable resistance to Nazism in the officer corps, still traditional in outlook and dominated by the sons of Prussian nobility. Many officers were repelled by the cruelty and barbarism of the SS and Storm Troopers, and although loyal to Hitler as their commander in chief, they resented his lack of senior command experience. General Ludwig Beck, chief of staff of the Wehrmacht, felt strongly that many of Hitler's foreign policy decisions were dangerous and could lead to terrible consequences for Germany, but when he failed to convince his fellow commanders to join him in a coup against the Führer he resigned.

The one institution that might have had some success

in combating Nazi ideology was the Church. Nazi brutality toward Jews brought widespread criticism from Christian church leaders in other countries, and it was due to this support that the Catholic Church and the various Protestant denominations were able to resist incorporation into a state-controlled agency responsible for church affairs. Individual pastors like Martin Niemöller and Dietrich Bonhoeffer spoke out boldly against Nazi anti-Semitism and racist theories from their pulpits; they would later be arrested and Bonhoeffer executed in World War II, an early martyr in the cause of freedom and human rights. But as an institution, the Church as a whole allowed itself to be stifled and manipulated in the same manner as the universities and the schools.

DRANG NACH OSTEN

The Drang Nach Osten, or "March to the East," formed the core of Hitler's foreign policy. His goal was to build up German military strength to enable the nation to expand at the expense of its neighbors, especially those to the east, providing more "living space" for Germany's growing population. To reach this goal, it was necessary to get around the limits on German manpower and rearmament imposed by the Versailles Treaty. In 1936, Hitler announced a Four-Year Plan designed to convert industries to arms production and make the country self-sufficient in food production. When other European countries warned that rearmament would violate the terms of the treaty, Germany withdrew from the League

At a 1936 Nazi Congress, Hitler deplores Germany's land shortage, while expressing envy for Russia's abundant resources.

of Nations and Hitler declared that it would no longer be bound by treaty terms.

With the rearmament program well under way, the Führer decided to "test the waters." In 1936, German troops marched into the Rhineland, a border province that had been demilitarized after the war. German armies were weaker than those of Britain and France at that point, and a show of force by either country might well have compelled German troops to withdraw. But nothing happened; a moment that might have changed the course of history passed uneventfully.

Hitler's eastward march went into high gear in 1938 and 1939. Austria was the first addition. Aside from Hitler's own blood ties, the affinity was natural. Furthermore, the Nazis had established a strong branch in Vienna which was agitating for Anschluss (union) with Germany. Pressured on all sides, the Austrian government held a referendum. The vote was 99 percent in favor of Anschluss. German troops moved to secure Austria's borders with other countries, and Hitler returned in triumph to Vienna, the city he had left a quarter of a century earlier.

Hitler's next goal was Czechoslovakia, Germany's southeastern neighbor. The country had been independent only since World War I, and, in addition to its two main ethnic groups—the Czechs and the Slovaks—it had a large German population in the Sudetenland, a border region. Local Nazi sympathizers had established a branch of the party there, and attacks by Czech soldiers on Sudeten Germans demonstrating for union of the province with Germany were sufficient for Hitler to claim that they were being oppressed.

Unlike Austria, Czechoslovakia had a well-trained army, with strong border defenses and its own arms industry. It was also allied with Britain and France. However, Hitler did not believe that those countries would go to war over Czechoslovakia. It was far away, located inland within Germany's natural sphere of interest, and the British and French governments had publicly expressed a preference for peace over war. Hitler met with British prime minister Neville Chamberlain and French premier Edouard Daladier in Munich in late 1938 and solemnly assured them that once the Sudetenland was restored to it, Germany would have no further need to interfere in the affairs of its neighbors. Chamberlain and Daladier believed him, and went home to report that they had secured "peace in our time." The main victim of their preference for peace was Czechoslovakia. The Sudetenland was incorporated into Germany, and German forces set up a protectorate over the Czech region, while the Slovak population declared the independence of their region (as they have done again in 1992). Hitler boasted: "I have restored to the *Reich* the provinces stolen from us in 1919, restored the thousand-year-old unity of German *Lebensraum*, and I have striven to do all this without the horrors of war."[10]

WORLD WAR II

By 1939 the Nazis had been in power for six years. In practical terms, they had accomplished a great deal. Germany was again a strong military power and had expanded beyond its prewar borders to become the largest nation in central Europe. Despite his aggressive policies, many Germans believed that Hitler was a man of peace. A young girl expressed the prevailing mood of the time: "Hitler is a great man, sent to us from Heaven. Rumors of war are spreading rapidly but we do not worry; he is a man of peace and will settle things peacefully."[11]

Despite his pledge at Munich, Hitler was not yet finished with his march to the east. The next target was Poland. The port of Danzig (now Gdansk), formerly part of Germany, had been turned over to Polish administra-

British prime minister Neville
Chamberlain is cheered on his return
from Munich, as he displays a signed
"no war" document.

tion after World War I, although technically it was a free city. Now Hitler demanded its return. The Poles stood firm, confident in the support of their allies, Britain and France. But Hitler judged that they were no more likely to go to war over Poland than they had been over Czechoslovakia. The only country that might oppose a German advance into Poland, he felt, was the Soviet Union. After Jews, Communists ranked second on Hitler's list of enemies, and he and Soviet leader Joseph Stalin had sworn to destroy the other's regime. But self-preservation drew them together to sign a secret nonaggression treaty. Hitler now felt he could move against Poland without risking a war on two fronts, while Stalin gained time to prepare for what he still saw as an eventual confrontation with Germany.

On September 1, 1939, German armies swept across the Polish border without a declaration of war. Not only were they superior to Polish forces in equipment; they brought with them a new form of warfare, the *blitzkrieg*, or "lightning strike." Stuka dive-bombers and swift Messerschmitt fighter planes destroyed Polish aircraft on the ground, shot up airports, knocked out communications, and bombed cities. At the same time, mechanized Panzer armored units opened gaps in Polish defenses and advanced rapidly to encircle Polish ground forces. It was textbook warfare at its most efficient. The Polish army, made up mostly of cavalry on fine horses, and poorly equipped infantry, fought bravely. But it was no match for the German blitzkrieg and surrendered in less than a month.

The invasion brought a declaration of war on Germany by Britain and France; the Soviet Union observed the terms of the secret treaty and stayed neutral, taking over half of Poland as its price for neutrality. Subsequently, the war became a general European one as Italian dictator Benito Mussolini joined Hitler in declaring war on the democracies.

Hitler then launched his armies against other European countries, and again the blitzkrieg worked to perfection. Denmark and Holland surrendered in five days, Belgium in eighteen. Norway's turn came next, and in June 1940, France surrendered. Hitler traveled there personally to dictate peace terms to the defeated French, using as his temporary headquarters the same rickety wooden railroad dining car in which France's Marshal Ferdinand Foch had dictated peace terms to a defeated Germany in 1918. (The dining car is now in a museum.)

With the fall of France, Hitler assumed that the war was over. The only enemy left was the island nation of Britain. Hitler expected that the British would ask for peace negotiations. He wished to be allied with them anyway; together, Germany and Britain could rule the world. But Hitler knew very little about British character, and especially, once aroused, the British capacity for dogged persistence until they had "muddled through" and resolved a problem. Hitler knew even less about Winston Churchill, the prime minister who had replaced Chamberlain. When the British refused to negotiate, Hitler ordered his air force, the Luftwaffe, to bring them to their knees with massive bombing raids. But the bombings failed to break the British spirit. Eventually, the Royal Air Force threw back the Luftwaffe, and the land invasion Hitler planned for Britain, Operation Sea Lion, had to be indefinitely postponed.

With his plans to invade Britain blocked, Hitler and his generals formed another battle plan, Operation Barbarossa, a surprise invasion of the Soviet Union. On June 22, 1941, the anniversary of Napoleon's invasion of Russia in 1812, German armies launched a blitzkrieg against Soviet forces, contemptuously brushing aside the nonaggression treaty as they moved to complete Hitler's March to the East. But like Napoleon before him, Hitler misjudged his opponents as well as their terrain, climate, and capacity for resistance. He was confident that the speed and efficiency of the blitzkrieg would compensate for the difficulties of a Russian campaign. And the early results were spectacular. By October, German forces were within 14 miles (23 km) of Moscow. Soviet casualties were appalling; entire armies had surrendered, and most of the western Soviet Union, including the Ukraine, its largest and richest republic, was under German control.

In his excitement at the prospect of final victory, the Führer now made several critical mistakes. Against the advice of his generals, he ordered priority to be given to other military objectives. German forces were ordered to advance along the entire front rather than concentrate on the capture of Moscow, the Soviet capital. As a result, they were spread too thinly. Fresh Soviet manpower reserves stemmed their advance, and the Germans soon became bogged down in an unusually severe Russian winter, for which they were totally unprepared; Hitler had not even issued winter uniforms.[12]

Hitler's second mistake was to turn the Soviet civilian population, particularly the Ukrainians, against their conquerors. The Ukrainians hated Stalin, who had seized their lands, killed or exiled to Siberia thousands of Ukrainian farmers for opposing the land seizure, and turned their farms into huge, inefficient Russian-managed collectives. They welcomed German soldiers with the traditional gifts of bread and salt given to visitors, and were eager to help overthrow the Soviet dictator and also to kill Jews. But Hitler had given orders that not only Jews but also "racially inferior" Slavic peoples should be eliminated to provide living space for arriving German colonists sent to develop the "New Germany" of the Nazi future. Before long, the mistreatment and brutality of SS units toward the Ukrainians led to the rise of a resistance movement that harassed German forces on all sides.

Hitler's third, and in the long run his greatest, mis-

Adolf Hitler, Führer of the
United German Empire, Field Marshal
Hermann Göring, and Minister of
Propaganda Joseph Goebbels

take was to declare war on the United States. He did so after Japan, Germany's ally, had attacked the American naval base in Pearl Harbor, Hawaii. Like the Germans, the Japanese planned to expand their territories at the expense of their neighbors in order to meet the needs of their growing population. When the United States declared war on Japan, Hitler declared war in support of Japan. He knew very little about American character and even less about the American democratic process. He did not understand that on occasions of great danger a democratic nation could put aside its internal disagreements and the special interests of competing groups and mobilize all its resources against an enemy. The Führer now became the personal enemy of most Americans; popular songs urged people to "push his face in," and his thin face with mustache and drooping lock of hair became a familiar, detested sight on posters, billboards, and in newspaper photos. But far more significant was the total mobilization of American manpower and American industry to defeat the Reich. The war now became truly global, and the addition of American resources to those of Britain, France, and the Soviet Union ensured the eventual defeat of Hitler's Germany.

GÖTTERDÄMMERUNG

Wagner's opera *Götterdämmerung* ("Twilight of the Gods") had been Hitler's favorite since his days in Vienna. The theme of the gods going down to heroic defeat and death haunted him, and some scholars believe that he may have ordered the invasion of the Soviet Union as some sort of perverse death wish. As the tide of battle slowly turned against the German forces, this death wish became an obsession. Many years earlier, he had had his fortune told by pouring lead into cylinders in the fashion of medieval alchemists. This fortune told him he would die at the age of fifty-six. Ten days after his fifty-sixth birthday the prediction came true. As he sat in his underground bunker below the bombed-out Reichschancellery building in Berlin, he could hear the thunder of Soviet guns pounding the German defenses around the city's eastern perimeter. Reports told him that American forces had broken through on the Western Front and were nearing the Elbe. Hitler sensed that destiny had thrown him from its coattails. He had once said: "We are the last Germany. Should we ever go under there will be no Germany."[13]

On April 30, 1945, Adolf Hitler abandoned his people and the Third Reich he had brought briefly to power and then to tragic, mindless destruction. As Russian troops neared his bunker, fighting their way through bomb-blasted streets against teenage German soldiers who still believed in their Führer, he committed suicide. A week later, Germany surrendered. Its leaders were mostly dead by their own hands or in custody; the survivors would be tried later in a court in Nuremberg for war crimes, particularly the crime of genocide, the killing of an entire people. The Third Reich had blazed like a meteor across European skies and now was no more; the German nation's destinies lay in the hands of others.

THE HOLOCAUST

In his autobiographical novel *Das zebrochene Haus* (*The Broken House*) published in 1966, the German novelist Horst Kruger ends the book with the haunting epilogue: "This Hitler, he will stay with us to the end of our lives."[14] The main reason for the continuing impact of Hitler and the Nazis on German life nearly half a century after the dissolution of the Third Reich stems from the *Holocaust*. The word literally means a sacrifice by burning, but it is used specifically today to describe only one such sacrifice, the deaths—by various means, but mainly by gassing—of 6 million Jews in World War II at the hands of the Nazi regime. As noted earlier, anti-Semitism was a major element in Hitler's thought. Long before the deportations of Jews to the "death camps" began in 1942, he had written in *Mein Kampf*, referring to World War I: "If during the war twelve or fifteen thousand of these Hebrew corrupters of the people had been held under poison gas . . . the sacrifice of millions at the front would

A trainload of deportees—all old women
or mothers with children, therefore deemed
"useless for work"—arrive at the death
camp of Auschwitz in 1944.

not have been in vain." In 1939, in a speech to the Reichstag, he promised that the result of a world war "caused by international Jewish finance" would be the "destruction of the Jewish race in Europe."[15] By 1942, with most of Europe under German occupation (including the Jewish populations of the occupied countries), the stage was set for the Nazi "Final Solution" to the "problem" of the Jews, something that had preoccupied Hitler since his Vienna days.

The Final Solution envisaged the elimination of all Jews in Europe; they were to be rounded up and taken in sealed boxcars or cattle cars to concentration camps, and there either worked or starved to death or executed in gas chambers. Each camp had its ironic sign *Arbeit Macht Frei* ("Work Makes You Free") emblazoned over the entrance, and each death camp name—Auschwitz, Buchenwald, Dachau—brings today a sinister image of mass graves, bodies of skin and bone with no flesh, or "horse-drawn carts piled high with naked corpses," as a survivor of Dachau remembered.[16] The heaviest burden of the Final Solution fell on women and children. As one observer noted, "In the Nazi scheme of things there was a special design for Jewish children. Jews, including their children, must be eradicated as a matter of ideological necessity. The whole race must disappear, especially pregnant women and the young, the ideological roots of the Jewish people."[17]

It is this legacy from the Nazi past that continues to haunt Germany today. The "new," unified Germany still harbors anti-Semitic views—15 percent of the popula-

Concentration camp inmates were often worked or starved to death.

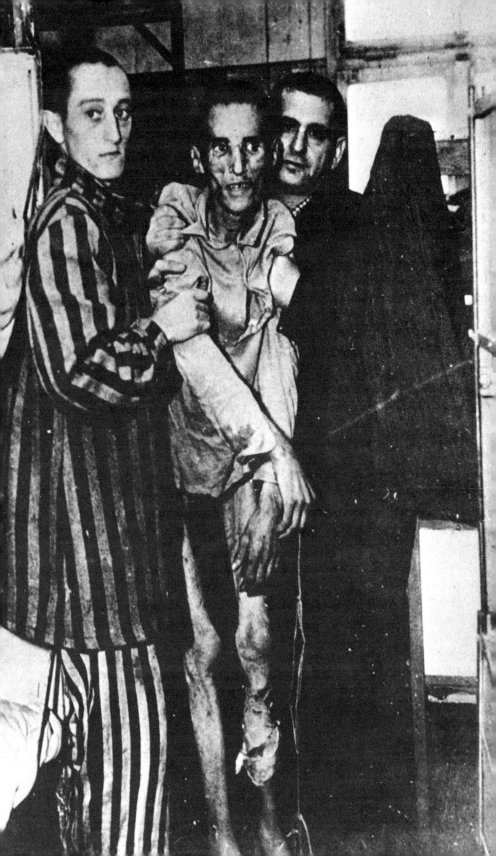

tion according to a 1988 poll—and in 1987 a West German general stated that the mass gassing of Jews was an example of efficiency. One possible reason for the survival of such views is that Jews and Germans are more alike than they are different, and they see each other in terms of competition. The leader of Germany's ultra-right-wing Republican Party observed that "Both Jews and Germans always want to be top of the class. The Germans want to be the best in everything. They are the best scholars—and the best murderers."[18] But these supposed similarities do not explain the Holocaust; nor do they explain the difficulties of the German people in confronting their Nazi past. A young German girl summed up the dilemma: "I know some facts. But I don't know much about my family during that period [of the Holocaust]. And I realize that, in my family, we do the same, like most German families, because of fear and a kind of guilt, we don't talk about it; that is how we deal with the past."[19]

SEVEN

THE
TWO GERMANYS

All the time they were creating
What has destroyed them,
And they fall with the burden
They built.
—Friedrich Junger,
Ultima Ratio

This grim epitaph of a distinguished German poet summed up Germany's situation in 1945. The Third Reich stood as a monument to self-destruction, Hitler's mad wish for Götterdämmerung in death and flames mirrored in its bombed-out cities, the desperate millions of refugees wandering across ruined Europe, the appalling images of emaciated survivors emerging from the death camps. The entire German land was now occupied by foreign powers. Six years of war had left 55 million dead, 4 million of them Germans; another 12 million ethnic Germans expelled from various parts of Europe arrived penniless in a land most of them had never seen, having lived all their lives somewhere else. The warnings of an American ambassador nearly thirty years earlier—". . . in the dark, cold northern plains of Germany there exists an autocracy deceiving a great people . . . preaching the virtue and necessity of war. And until that autocracy is either wiped out or made powerless there can be no peace on earth"[1]—seemed about to come true.

Yet the victors in war also faced a dilemma. What should be done with the defeated Reich? Although Germany lay prostrate, it was still the "Land in the Middle," the key to the balance of power in Europe. The four occupying powers were in general agreement that Germany should be permanently weakened but not dismembered. They were in agreement on almost nothing else. The Soviet Union, which had suffered most from German occupation, was determined to keep Germany from threatening its borders again, and to that end wished to establish "friendly" Communist-ruled governments in eastern Europe between German territory and its own. The United States, Britain, and France, increasingly suspicious of Soviet intentions, were equally determined to help Germany build a democratic system as a counterweight to Communism. As a result, not one but *two* Germanys arose from the ashes of defeat, the products of foreign political rivalries and ideological differences.

GERMANY DIVIDED

Initially, Germany was divided by the establishment of separate occupation zones, three in the western two-thirds of the country (French, British, and American, respectively) and a single Soviet-controlled zone in the eastern third. Berlin, still the capital but surrounded by the Soviet zone, became a separate occupation zone under joint four-power administration, with separate sectors for each of the occupying powers. (After 1947 this arrangement was simplified to one of separate administration of East and West Berlin under Soviet and American control respectively. It was this "divided" Berlin that the children who played in the Tiergarten on the day the Wall went up had known all their lives, the only Berlin they knew.)

At the Palace of Justice, in Nuremberg, Nazi
leaders including Hermann Göring, Rudolf Hess,
Joachim von Ribbentrop, and Wilhelm Keitel
(first row behind partition, from the left)
were tried and sentenced for war crimes.

The Potsdam Conference that set the rules for defeated Germany resulted in agreement on certain basic principles. Germany would be disarmed and demilitarized. The Nazi Party would be outlawed, along with all its auxiliary organizations. War criminals would be brought to justice in order to emphasize the German people's responsibility for the war. There was also general agreement that political life in Germany "should be reconstructed on a democratic basis; that all democratic parties should be encouraged, and education and the legal system reorganized. . . ."[2] But differences between the United States and its allies, and the Soviet Union precluded implementation of even these basic principles. In particular, the difference between Soviet and American understanding of "the democratic process" ensured Germany's division. German Communists led by Walther Ulbricht returned from exile and, with the backing of Soviet military forces, set about to outmaneuver other and more popular political parties in the eastern zone and establish a Communist regime.

Beginning in 1949, the division of Germany was formalized with the establishment of the Federal Republic of Germany ("West Germany") in the western zone and the German Democratic Republic ("East Germany") in the eastern zone. In this manner, and despite their apparent attachment to republicanism and democracy as indicated by their names, the two Germanys were far apart not only in terms of size and population, but also resources. As products of the Cold War between United States and Soviet systems of thought, politics, and economic and governmental administration that was to divide the world for nearly half a century, the two Germanys were also far apart in ideology.

WEST GERMANY

Integration of the Federal Republic into the Western democratic alignment of nations proceeded rapidly once the basic structure of the state had been established. In 1951 it became a member of the European Coal and Steel Community and the Council of Europe, and in 1954 the occupation was formally ended with the signing of the Treaties of Paris. Foreign forces were allowed to remain, but only under new agreements negotiated with the West German government. No longer were they there on German soil as occupiers. Subsequently, West Germany became a member of the North Atlantic Treaty Organization (NATO), the main defense organization against expected Soviet aggression in western Europe. By the end of the 1950s, the Federal Republic had been fully accepted into the democratic group of nations, with a stable political system, a successful economy, and a commitment to the democratic process that had been either lacking or ineffective in previous German regimes. But as Karl-Günther von Hase has noted, this commitment was in large part a reaction to the Third Reich. "There would be far more dissatisfaction with the political system if we didn't have the past to remind us. We would have more calls for order and strong men. We learned the hard way . . . that democracy is the worst form of government but for all the others."[3]

This Wyoming-size country (95,936 square miles, or 248,630 sq km, with a population more than ten times that of the Equality State) began what was presumed to be, at least in many German minds and certainly in those of the leaders of the democracies, a permanent existence with the establishment under Allied supervision of a federal political system. The system was codified in the 1949 constitution, which established a system of eleven *Länder* (states) plus two free cities, Hamburg and Bremen. One significant change in the new structure from the "old" Germany was the elimination of Prussia. East Prussia had been absorbed into Poland after the war, and the remaining Prussian lands were divided among several Länder.

The constitution also set up a new bicameral legislature, with a Bundesrat (senate) and a Bundestag (house of representatives) to replace the discredited institutions of the Third Reich. The Bundestag became the republic's chief lawmaking body; among its duties was the election of the chancellor (prime minister), and approval of the cabinet of ministers (similar to the British system). A Constitutional Court similar in form and function to the United States Supreme Court was formed to exert judicial control over laws passed by the Bundestag and to rule on the constitutionality of government actions.

The Federal Republic held its first Bundestag elections in 1949, with eight political parties nominating candidates. The Social Democrats, headed by Kurt Schumacher, a victim of the Nazi regime, were expected to win easily, being the best-established and the only party whose existence dated back to the Weimar Republic. But in a surprising turn of events, the Christian Democratic Union (CDU) won the majority of seats in the Bundestag, leaving the Social Democrats as a reluctant opposition. Theodor Heuss, head of the Free Democratic Party, allied with the CDU, was elected as the republic's first president (a largely ceremonial office), and Konrad Adenauer, the seventy-three-year-old founder of the CDU, became the first chancellor.

The "Adenauer era" in West Germany lasted from 1949 until 1963. Der Alte ("The Old Man"), as he was known to all Germans, proved a wise and farsighted leader. A devout Catholic and lifelong opponent of Hitler, he brought feuding Catholic and Protestant-dominated political parties together and included ex-Nazi officials in his government, thus avoiding the anger over Germany's defeat and loss of territory which had made possible Hitler's rise to power after World War I. He once said: "When you fall from the heights as we Germans have done, you realize that it is necessary to break with what has been. We cannot live fruitfully with false

Konrad Adenauer became chancellor of the
Federal Republic of Germany in 1949.

illusions."[4] Der Alte restored full independence and brought international respectability to West Germany. The Federal Republic's independence was recognized formally in 1955, and all occupation forces were withdrawn except for those in West Berlin. The capital was also moved from Berlin to Bonn, a quiet university town similar in many respects to Weimar. (Its previous distinction was that it was Beethoven's birthplace.) The move to Bonn had a special significance in that it separated political authority from the taint of Nazism still hanging over Berlin, and in any case, the former capital's location deep in the Soviet zone made it unusable.

WIRTSCHAFTSWUNDER

West Germany's political stability went hand in hand with economic recovery, each contributing to the other's success. American funds channeled through the Marshall Plan (named for United States secretary of state George C. Marshall) initiated the process. But it was the energy, discipline, organization, and hard work of the German people, the old virtues revived, that made possible a *Wirtschaftswunder*, an economic "miracle." Between 1950 and 1964, West Germany's gross national product (GNP), the standard index of a country's economic growth, tripled, largely due to the fact that partition had left the majority of manufacturing plants and other industries in the western zone. Adenauer and his portly, cigar-puffing finance minister, Ludwig Erhard, developed an economic formula that played an important role in the miracle.[5] They began with currency reform. Price controls were lifted, and a new currency, the deutsche mark, was introduced, its value stabilized through a new central bank, the Bundesbank. Because the government licensed the Bundesbank but did not control it, the deutsche mark soon became one of the world's most stable currencies.

Erhard's recovery plan combined free enterprise with

state control of certain institutions, such as the railroads, whose activities affected all Germans. An extensive package of welfare benefits plus high wages (the average German industrial worker earned 20 percent more than the British counterpart as recently as 1988) brought most West Germans affluence and leisure on an undreamed-of scale. A high level of production, exports, and domestic savings, the three barometers of economic growth, suggested to many people that the German tradition of expecting disaster to be just around the corner might finally be proven wrong.[6]

REFUGEES, GUEST WORKERS, AND DEMOCRACY

On the basis of longevity alone, West Germany could not be considered a fair-weather democracy, having outlived an empire, a republic, and Hitler's authoritarian Third Reich. With no single political party able to dominate the Bundestag, government for most of the period of West Germany's existence was by coalition. Far-right parties were unable to duplicate the Nazi success in the early years of the Weimar Republic, even in periods of recession, due to the innate conservatism of German voters and their general unwillingness to change the existing order. The National Democratic Party (NPD), which held nationalistic views similar to those of the Nazis but disclaimed Nazi connections, emerged in the 1960s to challenge the coalition. Having failed to win a seat in the Bundestag, it faded away as quickly as it had arisen. Student radicalism, terrorism sponsored by the Red Army Faction or by foreign terrorists and others fighting their battles on German soil during the 1970s, and even the Green movement, with its protests against nuclear energy and environmental degradation, were all taken pretty much in stride by the Federal Republic.

One area of national life in which German democracy has remained uncertain and incomplete involves the country's foreign community. Throughout its history, Germany has served as a land of refuge for many peoples, as well as a pathway for conquest. As noted earlier in this chapter, with the end of World War II, the refugee process accelerated. Millions of ethnic Germans expelled from other European countries washed across Germany's borders as those nations undertook a program of "ethnic cleansing"of their populations. The West German Basic Law recognized as "German" the descendants of persons of German stock residing within the borders of the 1937 Reich, as well as Germans from Eastern Europe who could prove that at least one grandparent was German. Consequently, Germany's neighbors (including the Soviet Union) rid themselves of a potential source of conflict, while the Federal Republic gained a population of skilled workers and professionals invaluable in the development of the economic miracle.

The supply of personnel dried up after the building of the Berlin Wall in 1961, and the West German government then began importing *Gastarbeiters* ("guest workers") from poorer countries such as Turkey, Yugoslavia, Portugal, and Greece to meet the continuing demand for cheap labor. By 1964 a million Gastarbeiters had come to take advantage of lucrative German labor contracts; the millionth, a Portuguese worker, was given a moped in a televised ceremony! In the 1970s and early 1980s, more and more Gastarbeiter families joined their breadwinners in Germany, and given the high immigrant birth rate, the percentage of foreign workers in the total population increased steadily. On the eve of reunification, about 7 percent (4.3 million) of the country's population were foreigners.

Politically, the foreign worker community is almost invisible—or was until reunification—having no representation and arousing little interest on the part of the West German press and media, and the public. The

"Guest" workers perform jobs undesirable to Germans. These Turkish laborers repair roads using materials that are hazardous.

German population has tended to regard the foreign workers and their families as social inferiors, so few efforts were made to integrate them into society, or to extend to them the political rights enjoyed by Germans. The largest single Gastarbeiter population, that of the Turks, has remained apart from the German majority due to the Germans' attitudes and social, linguistic, and religious differences despite the fact that two-thirds have lived in Germany for more than ten years and have few affinities with their homeland. As long as the Berlin Wall kept East Germans out of West Germany, Turks and other Gastarbeiters remained essential to the labor market, doing work that the West Germans did not want to do themselves. But as a 1988 report pointed out, "membership in an ethnic group signals acceptance of unqualified, repetitive, stressful and poorly paid work; it also signifies a poor knowledge of German, imperfect command of cultural standards, and only slight ability to adapt."[7]

THE GERMAN
DEMOCRATIC REPUBLIC

East Germany, the German Democratic Republic (DDR), included the balance of the territory of the Third Reich as of 1937, with a land area of 41,755 square miles (108,175 sq km) and a population of 17 to 18 million. One of its few distinctions during its forty-year existence (aside from relative longevity) was that it was the only country in Europe to *lose* population, due largely to a falling birth rate and large-scale emigration.

Article I of the DDR's constitution, approved in 1949, stated that "Germany is an indivisible democratic republic, composed of German states. The republic determines all matters that are essential to the existence and the development of the German people as a whole." However, it was not until 1972 that the two Germanys signed a treaty of mutual recognition and "good neighborly relations." The years of separation were marked by vast differences in political experience, economic development, social organization, and cultural values, and the very term *democracy* meant different things to East and West Germans.

The DDR, as mentioned earlier, came into existence as the result of the Soviet policy of ensuring Germany's division while also establishing Communist regimes in Eastern Europe. The Communists, led by Walther Ulbricht, seized power quickly with Soviet military backing and were able to discredit and then eliminate other and more popular political parties. With a handful of associates, Ulbricht, a good party boss although a poor speaker and totally lacking in charisma, ruled the republic with an iron hand for twenty-two years (1949–1971). During that period, he remade East Germany, the land of Goethe and Schiller, the beacon of German literature and culture, into the most Stalinist, the most Soviet, of the Soviet Union's East European satellite states. The DDR became almost totally dependent on the USSR in its economic system as well as its political organization. All industries were put under state control, initially to compensate the Soviet Union for war damages and subsequently to confirm the state's socialist nature. Farms were subdivided into plots and given to landless peasants or poor tenant farmers. As a result, a formerly productive agrarian economic system became stagnant, providing few jobs and forcing the government to import food.

Industry suffered equally under the heavy hand of state control. A ban on labor unions and the lack of any kind of fringe-benefits system for the work force, as well as growing anger over the privileges enjoyed by Ulbricht and the small group of party leaders in this supposedly classless society, led to a general strike by workers in 1953. It was the first such protest in Communist East German history, by those who were supposed to have benefited most from the Communist revolution. And it led to the predictable result. The government said that the strike was illegal and brought in Soviet tanks to patrol the streets and force the strikers back to work.

As we saw in the Prologue to this book, the building of the Berlin Wall marked a turning point in the relationship of the two Germanys. For the next thirty years, they were sealed off from each other as effectively as were the two halves of Berlin. Before the Wall, 2.5 million East Germans fled to West Germany through Berlin, inserting themselves into West German life, establishing careers, building families and personal relationships. After the Wall, for the next twenty-seven years the figure dropped to 616,000, most of whom seemed to have "hung on" in West Berlin. One observer wrote this about their general experience: "What happened to people in West Berlin was *hangengeblieben*. A friend went for a year in 1968, but then he stayed longer—*hangengeblieben*. A daughter departed for Berlin to study for four semesters, and now she still lives there, *hangengeblieben*. The word means 'stuck,' and calls up an image of a city of figures caught in a net, transfixed, gently floating . . . stuck in Berlin."[8] The freewheeling, consumer-oriented society of the Federal Republic contributed to this East German feeling of being "stuck" in a foreign land, one that was German in speech and street signs but unfamiliar in most other aspects of life.

Thirty years of isolation produced very different views of each other on the part of the two Germanys. West Germans viewed the DDR as a closed gray shell inhabited by people whom years of Communist control had made incapable of growth or change. The East Germans looked across the border at a society they were convinced was "stupid, money-distended, with its supermarkets, its portable TV sets, its pompous furniture." They felt that the Federal Republic was a Germany they no longer knew, a Germany where the old values of thrift, discipline, order, respect for authority, and moral uprightness no longer existed. As the years passed, the East Germans came to believe that they were the true heirs to the German nation, the preservers of the old Reich.[9]

In 1971 the aging Ulbricht was replaced under Soviet pressure by Erich Honecker, a lifelong Communist from a working-class background who had been jailed for ten years by the Nazis. Honecker brought some improvements into the lives of East Germans—more consumer goods, a low-cost housing program, loans to help newly married couples buy homes, maternity benefits for working mothers, and guaranteed welfare benefits for workers. But the country remained a police state, its population ruthlessly controlled by a vast network of *Stasis* (state security services) and informers who kept track of every citizen in huge files.

The contrast with the freewheeling Federal Republic was enormous, and Germans on both sides questioned whether unification could ever work. Helmut Schmidt, the Federal Republic's chancellor, observed in a 1979 speech: "The idea that one day a State of 75 million Germans could arise in the middle of Europe arouses concern in many of our neighbors. The German division is today part of the European balance of power . . . in Europe."[10] Many Germans agreed with him. A resident of a town cut in half by an "Iron Curtain," a chrome, wire, and steel barrier with a 3-mile (5 km) "exclusion zone" filled with mines and detection devices on the eastern side, said: "A reunited Germany would be too big for either the U.S. or the Soviet Union; none of them want us together."[11] And as recently as 1990, Günter Grass, West Germany's most distinguished living novelist, warned: "Don't unify Germany; there can be no demand for a new version of a unified nation that in the course of seventy-five years filled the history books with suffering, rubble, millions of refugees, millions of dead, and the burden of crimes that can never be undone."[12]

EIGHT

AND
THEN THERE
WAS ONE

Germany is not an island. . . .
No other country is in the same degree,
woven actively or passively into the
world's destiny.
—Oswald Spengler,
Jahre der Entscherdung

Abruptly, in 1989–90, the "German problem" returned
to center stage in Europe as the Berlin Wall came crash-
ing down along with the rest of the "Iron Curtain" that
had divided the two Germanys. As late as October 1989,
unification of East and West Germany was still considered unthinkable by most European leaders as well as
the heads of state of both Germanys. An East German
Socialist Party leader stated the issue unequivocally in a
radio broadcast: "The German Democratic Republic is
only conceivable as an anti-Fascist socialist state, as a
socialist alternative to the Federal Republic."[1] Forty years
of parallel existence had taken its toll; in 1987, East
Germany's Erich Honecker (who had been responsible
for the building of the Berlin Wall in his former capacity
as minister for state security) became the first DDR head

132

of state to pay an official visit to the Federal Republic, and in a well-publicized interview he predicted that the Wall would last 100 years.

Both Honecker and the Wall were gone in November 1989, barely a month after leaders of the East European nations had convened in Berlin to honor Honecker's seventeen years in power and the DDR's fortieth anniversary. Despite the pomp and ceremony of the occasion, there were omens of what was to come. Mikhail Gorbachev, the Soviet leader, is said to have warned Honecker in a private conversation that "history punishes those who come late to it."[2] In any case, Gorbachev's reversal of the policies of his predecessors supplied the motivation and mechanisms for the German revolution that overthrew Honecker and his government. Early in 1989, Gorbachev announced a new Soviet policy of *glasnost*, or openness, intended not only to improve relations with the non-Communist world but also to revitalize Soviet society. At the same time, admitting in effect the Communist system's failure to meet national goals and public needs, Gorbachev set in motion a policy of *perestroika*, or restructuring, for the Soviet economy. Although glasnost and perestroika eventually swept Gorbachev and his government from power, they had an even greater effect on Eastern Europe and especially on East Germany.

With the fortieth anniversary celebrations at hand, the sequence of events in the "October Revolution" took on a momentum of their own. Crowds in East Germany brought out to applaud the regime and its accomplishments protested instead, shouting slogans such as "Help us, Gorby" and "Glasnost and perestroika here, too." The demonstrations were broken up, but the damage had already been done, the regime discredited.

This unexpected turn of events was greatly enhanced as East Germany's neighbors began opening their borders. One after another, Communist regimes that had been in

In 1989 Soviet president Mikhail
Gorbachev stood with East German leader
Erich Honecker, but his message of
glasnost was to contribute to
the downfall of Honecker's regime.

power for nearly half a century toppled under popular pressure. Record numbers of East Germans wanting "out" of the DDR crossed the open borders into Hungary and Austria, where they were given bus tickets and sent on to West Germany. As *Aussiedler* (settlers), they were entitled to automatic citizenship in the Federal Republic and were guaranteed 100 marks plus unlimited job opportunities to begin life over.

This sudden mass exodus widened the gulf between the government and the people in the DDR.[3] But the millions of East Germans who remained, accomplished an even greater feat, the overthrow of a repressive regime without violence or foreign military aid. The turning point came in the city of Leipzig, where police and heavily armed Stasis confronted some 70,000 unarmed citizens shouting *"Wir sind das Volk!"* ("We are the people!"), the rallying cry of what became known as the German "October Revolution," and backed down, many of them even joining the demonstrators. From then on, the DDR regime's days were numbered. Honecker resigned and fled into exile in the Soviet Union.[4] His successor, Egon Krenz, failed in last-minute efforts to reorganize the ruling Socialist Party and placate the opposition. By the end of October, the Leipzig demonstrators had grown to half a million, while crowds in other East German cities marched, demanding freedom of speech and assembly and free elections and shouting "We are the people, we're staying here" in a heady display of revolutionary spirit.

DOWN COMES THE WALL

It was November 9, 1989, the fifty-first anniversary of Kristallnacht, the "Night of Broken Glass" that marked the launching of Hitler's full-scale persecution of the Jews. But this November 9 produced a very different result. No one knows for sure who gave the order, or indeed if there even was an order. But in a sort of spontaneous dance of life, Ossis and Wessis alike flocked to the Berlin Wall and, working together, brought it tumbling down. Some climbed on top of it, others chipped away with hammer, chisel, knife, and pickax until der Mauer resembled a block of Swiss cheese. People danced on it, embraced, exchanged flowers; whole families were reunited at the Wall. "It was a magical moment," wrote an eyewitness. "The possession of a city by its people, under a full moon, transforming the cruelest urban landscape into a scene of hilarity and hope."[5]

The fall of the Wall not only brought a surge of Ossis into West Berlin; it also inaugurated the rebirth of a united Germany. Unification required barely a year to complete. In March 1990, elections were held for a new East German parliament—the first freely elected body in DDR history. The former Communist Party, now reorganized as the Party for Democratic Socialism, competed for seats with a number of newly formed non-Communist parties, with the balance going to a coalition of parties calling itself the Alliance for Germany. The new parliament had already committed itself in its platform to unity with West Germany, and in July 1990 the two legislative bodies agreed to form an economic, social, and currency union. Formal unification went into effect in October, and the DDR was metamorphosed into five Länder (states) in the new Federal Republic of Germany. In Berlin, revelers gathered at the historic Brandenburg Gate, the ancient entrance to the city, on New Year's Eve, throwing firecrackers at each other's feet, popping champagne, and singing drinking songs with arms linked beer-hall style, their walled world now unwalled, their world turned *Wansinn* ("upside down," "crazy").

POSTSCRIPT

Three years after formal reunification, the path being followed by the Federal Republic remains unclear. The

*November 1989:
At Berlin's historic
Brandenburg Gate—a
symbol of the
country's painful
division—thousands
of West German citizens
gather as East German
border guards stand
atop the Wall.
Right: A demonstrator
pounds away, to begin the
work of dismantling it.*

national mood is best described as "cranky," as the nation continues to stumble along economically. A sharp rise in violence against foreigners, both those long resident in the country and newly arrived refugees seeking asylum in 1991–1993 has polarized German society, with many persons, and particularly unemployed youth, blaming their problems on the large foreign work force. And the basic differences between East and West Germans brought about by forty years of political separation and contrasting economic and social systems have proved more difficult to bridge than expected. The government's inability to ensure a smooth economic transition and deal effectively with right-wing neo-Nazi groups responsible for the violence gave rise to a new term, coined in the German-language fashion, to describe the popular mood—*Politikverdrossenheit*, or "fed up with politics as usual."

One positive sign for the future is Germany's continued strong commitment to European unity. Foreign Minister Hans-Dietrich Genscher formally renounced all territorial claims on the country's neighbors in a 1991 speech, saying: "The dark chapters of our history are a cause for reflection on what was done in Germany's name. That will not be repeated."[6] The government of Chancellor Helmut Kohl has taken the lead in approving the Maastricht Treaty, which will bring into existence a single European Community, arguing in 1993 that its headquarters be in Berlin, and that the German mark be the standard for a single European currency because of its strength against other currencies.

The political stability of the republic, inherited in large part from the West German state, is another positive step on the way to Germany's maturity. The West German constitution was adopted as the law of the land for Germany, and a single all-German Bundestag took office in 1991. Kohl's Christian Democratic Union

(CDU) won 54 percent of the seats, governing by coalition with the Socialist Party (SPD), the major opposition party. The former East German Communist Party, renamed the Party of Democratic Socialism, was almost shut out in the voting. In June, the new Bundestag approved in a close vote (337–320) the return of the German capital from Bonn to Berlin.[7] Despite its symbolic associations with the divided German past, the Nazis, and two world wars begun by German arrogance, Berlin holds a special place in German minds as a symbol of that elusive unity that has haunted Germans almost since they emerged in history as a people, trailing behind their neighbors and constituting what some writers have called the "retarded nation."

Despite his years in office—eight as head of West Germany and two at the helm of the Federal Republic—and his success in bringing the two Germanys together, Kohl's popularity plummeted drastically in 1992–93. In an October 1992 poll, 65 percent of those queried said he should be replaced. The bulk of the criticism (helping to explain why so many Germans have become *Politikverdrossenheit*) concerned his government's handling of the economy and the related issue of antiforeign violence. Like U.S. president George Bush, Kohl had promised "no new taxes" upon taking office. But in July 1991, the heavier-than-expected costs of unification forced a 7.5 percent increase in the already high income tax, along with steep increases in taxes on gasoline, telephones, and other essential services. A year later, with the economy still in recession, Kohl warned that another tax increase would be inevitable by 1995. He said that the cost of servicing East German foreign debts of $266 billion and converting former state-managed industries in the eastern region to efficient, pollution-free production left him without any alternatives.[8]

These economic difficulties were indirectly responsi-

Chancellor Helmut Kohl speaks
at a news conference in front of
a poster heralding "the future."

ble for a huge increase in violence against foreigners, with 17 dead in 3,000 separate incidents in 1992 and 1993. Traditionally, and especially since World War II and during the Cold War period, western Germany has been a land of asylum for refugees. Article 16 of the West German constitution adopted by the republic after unification established the right of asylum (*asyl*) for all persons fleeing political persecution. It was written specifically to compensate for Nazi racial policies during the period of the Third Reich, when thousands of persons were forced to leave because of their religious or political beliefs or their non-Aryan backgrounds. During the period of Germany's division, the flow of refugees remained small. But a large and ever growing number of foreigners were allowed to enter West Germany on work contracts as Gastarbeiters (guest workers) in the 1960s and 1970s because they were needed to fill jobs opening up in the German economic expansion.

During the economic boom, both guest workers and Germans profited. Many of the Gastarbeiters sent for their families and settled permanently as non-voting members of German society. It was even said that during this period there were more Turks in Berlin than in the largest Turkish city, and more Italians in German industrial areas than in the Italian industrial city of Turin. By 1990, foreigners made up 7 percent of Germany's population—Turks, Italians, Portuguese, Spaniards, and others from as far away as Vietnam and the Philippines.

The economic downturn of the 1980s, and the high costs of reunification, have posed a double problem for the government. On the one hand, unstable conditions in eastern Europe led to a great increase in persons seeking asylum. Over 2 million persons have entered the country claiming political refuge since 1989. Under German law, anyone presenting himself or herself at a border crossing point and using the magic word *Asyl* had the right to stay in Germany, receiving all the social benefits and welfare assistance of the German state until the case had been decided. In practice these benefits, averaging $250 per month for a family of four, plus meals and housing, have cost the government $6 billion a year, a further burden on a country already weighed down by the higher-than expected costs of unification.

With asylum seekers pouring across Germany's borders in ever-increasing numbers, and in some cities taking over entire apartment buildings, anti-foreign violence spread. The worst aspects of German character were evident as neo-Nazi groups began attacking foreigners. In August 1992, it reached a peak as gangs of unemployed young men in black leather jackets and swastika armbands, armed with clubs and knives, rampaged through a hundred cities and towns shouting "Germany for the Germans!," "Heil Hitler!" and carrying placards with such slogans as "The Fourth Reich Lives on the Corpse of the Third." In the port city of Rostock, residents cheered as the youths attacked and firebombed a hostel housing several hundred asylum seekers, mostly Romanians and Vietnamese. There were a number of casualties. A busload of Danish Boy Scouts was assaulted near the border, and in downtown Dresden the "skinheads" (so called because of their scalped appearance) marched four abreast through city streets shouting "Foreigners out! We'll get all of you!"

The violence, directed initially at those seeking asylum, because of fears that the foreigners would take jobs away from "good" Germans, increasingly turned against the Gastarbeiters in late 1992 and 1993. The firebombing of an apartment building in the small city of Moelln, near Hamburg, in which three members of a Turkish family resident for thirty years and well liked in the community died, indicated that in the minds of the neo-Nazis no foreigner should feel safe in Germany any longer; the Gastarbeiters were now unwelcome guests.

A neo-Nazi march through
the streets of Dresden

As the violence intensified, the majority of the population reacted strongly, as law-abiding Germans of all ages denounced the extremists and demanded government action to control them. The older generation, with painful memories of the Third Reich, criticized them as *Fremdenfeindlichkeit*, a German word meaning "hostile toward strangers," and thus acting in an unacceptable manner. Young people have been equally critical. "I am really ashamed to be German," said a Berlin high school student after a firebombing incident. "First there were right-wing people who throw stones at refugees, and now left-wing people attack politicians. People all over the world will think that there are no sensible people in Germany." Another student complained: "The U.S. newspapers see only these 300 extremists. They don't see the 350,000 who want peace." "They [the neo-Nazis] are less intelligent," said another girl scathingly. "Trade-school types. Primitive. Skinheads!"[9]

The government was also criticized for its failure to move forcefully against the neo-Nazis. After the Rostock firebombing, Romanians and other asylum seekers were removed from the city "for their own protection," and most of those arrested in connection with the violence received at most two- or three-year sentences. In December, after much equivocation, the government finally went into action, partly to quiet public criticism but also to improve its international image. Two neo-Nazi organizations, German Alternative and the Nationalist Front, were outlawed and their headquarters closed after police raids. A special mobile unit was formed to deal with the issue, and the state prosecutor announced that extremists would henceforth be treated as enemies of the state, with long prison terms for those convicted of anti-foreigner actions.

Public pressure increased and with 70 percent of the population favoring changes in Article 16, it seemed that the great majority of Germans agreed with Social Democratic leader Hans Klose that unrestricted immigration helped only right-wing rabble-rousers. Finally the Bundestag began debate on amendments to the asylum law. A new law was passed in May 1993, to take effect July 1. It would grant asylum only to refugees who could prove they were fleeing from war or oppression in their own countries. It seemed probable that most of the 350-400,000 refugees currently in the country would be expelled.

However the likelihood of a return to a Hitler-type "Germany for the Germans" remains remote. Foreign businesses, many of them developed by Gastarbeiters, are important to the economy. In 1992 alone, 33,000 Turkish-owned businesses generated 700,000 jobs and billions of marks in revenue. Also foreign workers continued to fill low-paying jobs such as garbage collecting, jobs most Germans are unwilling to do themselves.

Much has happened to the "Land in the Middle" and its people in the twenty centuries since Germania appeared as a vast, vaguely defined area on Roman maps. But many elements in the German character forged by the historical experience of these centuries survive. One element is that of work, particularly attitudes toward work and work performance. It is no accident that modern Germany has one of the best vocational-education training systems in the world. The instinct for order, cooperation, individually acceptable performance, and efficiency in production can be traced back as far as the medieval craft guilds. Its modern equivalent, the apprenticeship system, has outlived two world wars and has been a major factor in Germany's rise to become the leading economic power in Europe. Two thirds (1.8 million) of German young people are currently employed as apprentices by German firms (most of them with fewer than 500 employees). As

A crowd of about 100,000 people walk
through the Brandenburg Gate in a march
to protest anti-foreigner violence and
fascism. The large banner on the right
reads "I am a foreigner worldwide."

apprentices they are learning some 380 different trades. The result of this program, according to a recent book, is "the most highly skilled work force on the face of the earth, a youth unemployment rate lowest among the industrialized nations, and a sense of self-worth and competence among those starting out to work that would be the envy of Americans."[10] By the age of sixteen, German youth not headed for universities are spending up to four days a week at a job site learning such skills as bookkeeping, electrical engineering, plumbing, and auto mechanics. For every unemployed skinhead, there are probably a dozen serious young men and women busy building the country of the future.

It may well be this passion for order that continues to bind the German people to their past, while at the same time stretching them toward the future. Some scholars believe that German order, like German industriousness, sobriety, and other characteristics, was molded by the Thirty Years' War, in reaction to its disasters. Others argue that it is due to the country's late start in its effort to become a unified nation and compete economically. Whatever the origin, the German saying "Order is half of life" is still central to German life at the end of the twentieth century. One observer described German social life in these terms: "Be quiet in the afternoon. Yield to cyclists. Don't let your hedges grow too high. Open and close your shop when the government says. And don't dare name a child something the public records bureau doesn't like."[11] Even right-wing extremists observe the rules; a leaflet issued to members of one such group advised each one to carry a valid ID, car registration papers, pencil and paper, a pint of water, some food, and for women, birth-control pills and sanitary napkins, in the event of their arrest. It may be that the failure of security forces to break up the October 1989 Leipzig demonstrations was due to their inherent German obedience to order. As a security policeman on duty at the time noted, "We saw that they were not a mob, they were entirely normal people, who were shouting "Wir sind das Volk!" And we belonged to them too."[12]

One important feature of a successful democracy is *consensus*—the ability of groups with different and often opposing interests to work together for the common good. The West German republic was successful in doing so; consensus helped to carry it through half a century of struggles and problems. But one fourth of the population of unified Germany has had no experience with democracy or its economic equivalent, capitalism. Thus this "new" nation in an old land faces a twofold challenge. The first challenge is how to bring a population that has known only state control by a repressive regime for five decades into harmony and consensus with the majority. The second challenge is how to rid German society of the ghosts of the past, ghosts that keep surfacing. These ghosts—of Hitler, the Holocaust, ancient racial and religious hatred—must be dealt with in German minds if this new Germany is to hold an important place in the emerging united Europe, and is to work effectively with the United States and other countries in shaping the new world order. The task must begin at home; it is a difficult one, but not impossible given the great strengths of the German people.

SOURCE NOTES

PROLOGUE

1. The name is American military terminology. There were three entry points in all. Checkpoints Alpha (A) and Bravo (B) were entry points to West Berlin from East Germany. Checkpoint Charlie (C) was the third, the only one within the city.

2. Coleman Andrews, "Berlin: Both Sides Now," *Metropolitan Home*, May 1990, p. 82.

3. Peter Wyden, *Wall: The Inside Story of Divided Berlin* (New York: Simon and Schuster), 1989, p. 33.

CHAPTER 1

1. W. H. Riehl, *The Natural History of the German People*, trans. David Diephouse (Lampeter, Wales: Edwin Mellen, 1990), p. 106.

2. Anton Gill, *Berlin to Bucharest: Travels in Eastern Europe* (London: Grafton, 1990), p. 10.

3. F.R.H. Du Boulay, *Germany in the Later Middle Ages* (New York: Simon and Schuster, 1983), pp. 2–4.

4. Andreas Gryphius, quoted in Gordon A. Craig, *The Germans* (New York: Putnam, 1982), p. 20.

CHAPTER 2

1. Gordon A. Craig, *The Germans* (New York: Putnam, 1982), p. 22.

2. Ibid., p. 23.

3. Ibid., p. 25.

4. Diether Raff, *A History of Germany from the Medieval Empire to the Present*, trans. Bruce Little (Oxford, England: Berg, 1988), p. 76.

5. Hagen Schulze, ed., *Nation-Building in Central Europe* (Leamington Spa, England: Berg, 1987), p. 13.

CHAPTER 3

1. In his memoirs he wrote: "The teachers hated the nobility. My childhood was ruined for me at the Plamann Institute; whenever I looked out of the window and saw a team of oxen plowing I had to weep with homesickness." Quoted in Louis Snyder, *Diplomacy in Iron: The Life of Herbert von Bismarck* (Malabar, Fla.: Robert E. Krieger, 1985), p. 20.

2. Letter to Countess Karoline von Bismarck-Bohlen, quoted in Lothar Gall, *Bismarck* (London: Oxford University Press, 1987), p. 116.

3. Gall, ibid., p. 16.

4. Ibid., p. 131.

5. Ibid., p. 5.

6. Hans-Ulrich Wehler, *The German Empire 1871–1918*, trans. Ken Traynor (Leamington Spa, England: Berg, 1988), p. 53.

7. Ibid., p. 93.

8. Letter to Adolf Stoecker, quoted in Diether Raff, *A History of Germany from the Medieval Empire to the Present*, trans. Bruce Little (Oxford, England: Berg, 1988), p. 172.

CHAPTER 4

1. Warren B. Morris, *The Weimar Republic and Nazi Germany* (Chicago: Nelson Hall, 1982), p. 51.

2. Quoted in Ray Oldenburg, *The Great Good Place* (New York: Paragon House, 1989), p. 92.

3. Hans Seemuller, quoted in Timothy W. Ryback, "Report from Dachau," *The New Yorker*, August 3, 1992, p. 54.

4. Speech to the Reichstag, 1911, quoted in Diether Raff, pp. 211–212.

5. Felix Gilbert, *A European Past: Memoirs 1905–1945* (New York: Norton, 1988), p. 32. The writer recalled being sent to

school with a piece of this bread for his lunch, spread with some kind of smeary paste. "I tried feeding it to the seagulls, but even they would not eat it."

6. Quoted in Raff, p. 228. Reinhardt later served as chief of staff of the Army during the Weimar Republic.

7. Details in Morris, p. 51.

8. Theo Hupfauer, in Johannes Steinhoff, Peter Pechel, and Dennis Schowalter, eds., *Voices from the Third Reich: An Oral History* (Washington, D.C.: Regnery Gateway, 1989), p. xxvi.

CHAPTER 5

1. The swastika, or hooked cross, an ancient symbol of unknown origin, was often associated with sun worship and among early Christians with Christ, "sun of righteousness." It is found in the art of many cultures: American Indian, Hindu, Buddhist, etc.

2. Joachim Fest, *Hitler*, trans. Richard and Clara Winston (New York: Harcourt Brace, 1974), p. 118.

3. John Toland, *Hitler: The Pictorial Documentary of His Life* (Garden City, N.Y.: Doubleday & Co., Inc., 1978), p. 2.

4. Peter Broner, *Night of the Broken Glass* (Barrytown, N.Y.: Station Hill, 1991), p. 58. The comments are made by a character in a novel, but they reflect accurately the mood of the period.

5. His friend "Putzi" Hanfstaengl commented: "Only a few yards away was a young woman, her eyes fastened on the speaker. Transfixed, she was completely under the spell of Hitler's despotic faith in Germany's future greatness." Quoted in Norman Stone, *Hitler* (Boston: Little, Brown and Co., 1980), pp. 9–10.

6. Ian Kershaw, *The Hitler Myth: Image and Reality in the Third Reich* (Oxford, England: Clarendon, 1987), p. 22.

7. David Irving, *Göring: A Biography* (New York: Morrow and Co., Inc., 1989), p. 45.

8. Hess later fled Germany early in World War II and parachuted into England in a vain attempt to bring a prompt end to the war. One associate described him as having "a tuneless whistle and deep-sounding banalities; he had buck teeth and always avoided frontal photographs." Toland, p. 16.

9. Joseph W. Bendersky, *A History of Nazi Germany* (Chicago: Nelson Hall, 1985), p. 160.

10. Alexander Reissner, *Berlin 1675–1945: Rise and Fall of a Metropolis* (London: Oswald Wolff, 1984), p. 146.

CHAPTER 6

1. Henry M. Pachter, *Modern Germany: A Social, Cultural, and Political History* (Boulder, Colo.: Westview, 1978), p. 201.

2. Kershaw, p. 66.

3. Joahannes Steinhoff, Peter Pechel, and Dennis Showalter, eds., *Voices from the Third Reich: An Oral History* (Washington, D.C.: Regnery Gateway, 1989), p. xxix.

4. The decree mandating the salute stated: "Anyone not wishing to come under suspicion of negative behavior will render the German Greeting [that is, *Heil Hitler*]." Wilhelm Fischer observed that "before 1933, the Nazis' comical salute was considered a joke. But we soon stopped laughing." Ibid., p. xxxvi.

5. See Kenneth Baker, "When the Nazis Took Aim at Modern Art," *Smithsonian* 22, no. 4 (July 1991). A new exhibit of the same show was shown in the United States in 1991.

6. Comment by Albert Bastian, in Steinhoff et al., p. 15.

7. Fritz Stern, *Dreams and Delusions: The Drama of German History* (New York: Knopf, 1987), p. 135.

8. Martin Gilbert, *Atlas of the Holocaust* (Oxford, England: Pergamon, 1988), p. 72.

9. Amity Shlaes, *Germany: The Empire Within* (New York: Farrar, Straus, 1991), p. 59, quoting the leader of the Social Democrats in Bavaria. His hometown was "a town that hated the Nazis."

10. Quoted in Diether Raff, p. 294.

11. Kershaw, p. 142.

12. Germany issued a special medal to survivors of the 1941–42 winter campaign. The recipients called it cynically *Gefrierfleischorden* ("the frozen-meat medal").

13. As early as 1933, Hermann Keyserling had commented on the phenomenon "of the German nation, which has always been in love with death and to whom the tribulations of the Nibelungs are a constantly recurring experience." Hans Kessler, *Diaries of a Cosmopolitan*, p. 461.

14. David Marsh, *The Germans: The Pivotal Nation* (New York: St. Martin's, 1989), p. 11.

15. *Cf.* Linda Joffee, in *Christian Science Monitor*, August 18, 1992.

16. Timothy W. Ryback, "Report from Dachau," *The New Yorker*, August 3, 1992, p. 55.

17. George Eisen, *Children and Play in the Holocaust: Games*

Among the Shadows (Amherst: University of Massachusetts, 1988), p. 13. Liberators of the inmates of the Theresienstadt camp found children's poems and drawings with sad epitaphs like "There are no butterflies here, in the ghetto."

18. Marsh, pp. 218–219.

19. Joffee.

CHAPTER 7

1. James Gerard, *My Four Years in Germany* (New York: 1917), p. 317.

2. Walter Laqueur, *Europe in Our Time: A History, 1945–1992* (New York: Viking, 1992), p. 99.

3. Interview quoted in David Marsh, *The Germans: The Pivotal Nation* (New York: St. Martin's, 1989), p. 28. The observation about democracy was originally Winston Churchill's.

4. Quoted in Gordon A. Craig, *The Germans* (New York: Putnam, 1982), p. 45.

5. Erhard's motto was *"Wohlstand für Alle"* ("Prosperity for All"). In a 1954 speech, however, he downplayed his part in the "miracle," saying it was the result of "honest endeavor of a whole people."

6. "We Germans are always complaining about how terrible the world is. People are kept on their toes if they always think there is a disaster around the corner. You know that there's a way of avoiding it, provided you do your duty and work hard," Eberhard von Koerber, quoted in Marsh, p. 134.

7. Department of Political Science, Free University of Berlin, December 1988.

8. Amity Shlaes, *Germany: The Empire Within* (New York: Farrar, Straus, 1991), p. 217.

9. The DDR state railways kept the name of the prewar company, the Reichsbahn, set up in 1920, "as if the Empire were still waiting in the shunting-yard." Marsh, p. 149.

10. Quoted in Craig, p. 309.

11. Marsh, p. 319.

12. Günter Grass, "Don't Reunify Germany," *New York Times Magazine*, January 7, 1990.

CHAPTER 8

1. Otto Reinhold, quoted in David Marsh, *The Germans: The Pivotal Nation* (New York: St. Martin's, 1989), p. 111.

2. See David Halberstam, *The Next Century* (New York: Morrow and Co., Inc., 1991), p. 17.

3. An East German woman judge told an interviewer: "We didn't have socialism; we had a form of state capitalism, a system of exploitation with a very few party elite at the top." John Borneman, *After the Wall* (New York: Basic Books, 1991), p. 127.

4. In 1992 he was returned to Germany and went on trial on charges of manslaughter in the deaths of thirteen persons at the Wall during his regime. He remained unrepentant during the trial, saying at one point that the Wall had prevented World War III. Suffering from terminal liver cancer, the eighty-year-old ex-leader was released in January 1993 and given asylum in Chile.

5. Robert Darnton, *Berlin Journal 1989–1990* (New York: Norton and Co., Inc., 1991), p. 86.

6. Chancellor Helmut Kohl is said to view himself "as a modern-day Bismarck without the blood and iron." John Newhouse, "Sweeping Change," *New Yorker*, August 27, 1990, p. 85.

7. Government officials lobbied heavily to defeat the bill arguing that they preferred their tiny offices and charming cottages in the woods near the Rhine to the ugly Socialist ministry buildings inherited from the DDR in crowded, polluted Berlin.

8. A sign at the entrance to Bitterfield, a town in Saxony ringed by open coal pits and chemical plants, announces, Entering Emergency Environmental Area. It is considered to have the dirtiest air in all of Europe.

9. Danella Gross, in Mark Fritz, "Germany," AP dispatch, November 25, 1992.

10. Ray Marshall and Marc Tucker, *Thinking for A Living: Education and the Wealth of Nations*, quoted by Charles S. Clark, *Congressional Quarterly*, January 3, 1993.

11. Tyler Marshall, "Welcome to Germany's Rage to Order," *Los Angeles Times*, December 29, 1992.

12. Quoted in Elizabeth Pond, *Beyond the Wall: Germany's Road to Unification*. New York: Twentieth Century Fund, 1993, p. 118.

FOR FURTHER
READING

Borneman, John. *After the Wall*. New York: Basic Books, 1991.
A postunification study of German society by an ethnogra-
pher long resident in East Germany.

Broner, Peter. *Night of the Broken Glass*. Barrytown, N.Y.: Station
Hill Literary Editions, 1991. A novel depicting with extraor-
dinary realism the events that led up to Kristallnacht, exam-
ined in the relationships of several German and Jewish
families.

Craig, Gordon. *The Germans*. New York: Putnam, 1982. An
informal political, social, and intellectual history by a distinguished historian.

Darnton, Robert. *Berlin Journal 1989–1990*. New York: Norton,
1991. A firsthand account of the toppling of the Wall and
subsequent events.

Dwork, Deborah. *Children with a Star: Jewish Youth in Nazi Europe*.
New Haven, Conn.: Yale University, 1991. A child psychol-
ogist's vivid accounts of Jewish children's lives under Nazism.

Fest, Joachim. *Hitler*. Trans. Richard and Clara Winston. New
York: Harcourt Brace, 1974. The standard biography, rich
in detail and insights.

Gall, Lothar. *Bismarck*. London: Oxford University, 1987. The
definitive biography.

Hitler, Adolf. *Mein Kampf*. Trans. Ludwig Love. New York:
Stackpole, 1939. The first English-language edition. Includes

Hitler's foreword, written while he was in prison for the Beer-Hall Putsch.

Kershaw, Ian. *The Hitler Myth: Image and Reality in the Third Reich.* Oxford, England: Clarendon, 1984. Analyzes how and why the "image" of the Nazi leader was packaged and sold to the German people.

Marsh, David. *The Germans: The Pivotal Nation.* New York: St. Martin's, 1990. A comprehensive study by the chief correspondent of the *London Financial Times.*

Morris, Warren B., Jr. *The Weimar Republic and Nazi Germany.* Chicago: Nelson Hall, 1982. A well-written history of the period up to Germany's war defeat.

Pachter, Henry M. *Modern Germany.* Boulder, Colo.: Westview, 1978. A useful and informative general history packed with interesting anecdotes.

Pond, Elizabeth. *Beyond the Wall: Germany's Road to Unification.* New York: Twentieth Century Fund, 1993. A thorough, well-written account of the 1989–90 unification, based on extensive interviews. The author, a journalist, was in Germany at the time.

Rubenstein, Richard L., and Roth, John K. *Approaches to Auschwitz: The Holocaust and its Legacy.* Atlanta, Ga.: John Knox, 1987. A thoughtful study by two theologians of the antecedents and development of anti-Semitism and its culmination in the Holocaust.

Shlaes, Amity. *Germany: The Empire Within.* New York: Farrar Straus, 1991. An account by a journalist and *Wall Street Journal* correspondent of German attitudes and views in the wake of reunification.

Turner, Henry Ashby. *The Two Germanys Since 1945.* New Haven, Conn.: Yale University, 1987. A general history of the post–World War II period.

Wyden, Peter. *Wall: The Inside Story of a Divided Berlin.* New York: Simon and Schuster, 1989. A perceptive account of the lives of children and their families living in proximity to the Berlin Wall, before its construction and during the years of its existence.

INDEX